THE ECONOMICS
OF SAINTHOOD

The author with friends.

THE ECONOMICS
OF SAINTHOOD

Religious Change
among the Rimrock Navajos

Kendall A. Blanchard

RUTHERFORD • MADISON • TEANECK
FAIRLEIGH DICKINSON UNIVERSITY PRESS
LONDON: ASSOCIATED UNIVERSITY PRESSES

© 1977 by Associated University Presses, Inc.

Associated University Presses, Inc.
Cranbury, New Jersey 08512

Associated University Presses
Magdalen House
136–148 Tooley Street
London SE1 2TT, England

Library of Congress Cataloging in Publication Data

Blanchard, Kendall, 1942–
The economics of sainthood.

Bibliography: p.
Includes index.
1. Navaho Indians—Religion and mythology.
2. Navaho Indians—Missions.
3. Navaho Indians—Economic conditions.
4. Indians of North America—Religion and mythology—Southwest, New.
5. Indians of North America—Southwest, New—Missions.
6. Indians of North America—Southwest, New—Economic conditions.
I. Title.
E99.N3B54   301.5'1'0978983   75–10141
ISBN 0–8386–1770–0

To my mother,
Lois Blanchard Eades,
for never letting me forget the
importance of the "right word"

Contents

7

List of Tables

9

Preface

This is the study of the interrelationships of religious change and economic behavior within a small Navajo community in New Mexico called *Rimrock*.* Specifically, it is a reevaluation of Weber's classic Protestant-ethic hypothesis in a non-Western context.

Among the Rimrock Navajos over the past several decades, there has been a significant tendency for increasing economic rationalism—as this is defined from a Western capitalistic perspective—to accompany novel religious behavior at both individual and household levels. Sainthood, the participation in one of the two protestant-mission programs in the area (Nazarene and Mormon), appears related to quantifiable financial advantage : better jobs, greater mobility, and higher wages.

However, in contrast to the atmosphere of sixteenth-century Europe, the cultural climate in Rimrock has yet to experience anything resembling ideological revolution. While evangelical Protestantism has been marketing its message in the area for over thirty years, the so-called Navajo converts have yet to internalize its novel language and foreign doctrinal propositions.

* The name *Rimrock* is a pseudonym, as are all names used for persons still alive and living in the Rimrock area.

11

Despite the zeal of ambitious missionaries and their assertions to the contrary, the Bible carriers among The People (from Diné, the term Navajos use for referring to themselves as a group) have instead developed syncretic belief systems that conveniently combine compatible elements of both the new and old. This is the extent of the presumed ideological change.

The economic differentials associated with sainthood in Rimrock are explicable only in light of the very practical and immediate benefits accruing to mission participation; there is no theological transformation. Increased opportunities for education, closer ties with the local, white power-structure, and direct distribution of material goods are just a few of the options available to church-going Navajos. These advantages have had a positive effect on the economic status of the saints, relative to that of their more traditional neighbors.

The Weberian concept of the Protestant ethic, with its idolization of hard work and stern censorship on sensual license, is of no value in the attempt to understand the obvious correlation between religious and economic change among the Navajo mission groups in Rimrock. This is the book's major hypothesis.

This work also describes contemporary Navajo life in Rimrock. No complete anthropological investigation of The People's culture in the area has been undertaken since 1950 (*see* Introduction). A critical survey of the changing patterns in the region as of the 1970 period appears timely.

The Introduction of the book is a background study of the Rimrock area and its residents. It also contains a short history of local anthropological inquiry and a discussion of sociological theory pertinent to the hypotheses to be tested in the ensuing analysis. Chapter one is a thorough overview of Rimrock Navajo history, culture, and patterns of change. Chapter two is a description of Protestant-missionary activity among the Indian population in the Rimrock area. Chapter three is an analysis of the economy, its recent changes, trends, and a comparison of the economic behavior of the two major ideological factions among the Rimrock Navajos—the church and the unchurched (traditional)—while chapter four is a critical investigation of the significant differentials evident in the comparison. The final chapter is a summary and projection of Protestantism's role in the future of Rimrock-Navajo life.

This study is based on approximately eighteen months of field work conducted in Rimrock during the period between June 1970 and August 1973. During this time I lived in the area, working with both Navajos and Anglos. I completed many social census forms, eliciting information concerning kinship, job history, mobility, marriage, children, education, language ability, travel experience, income, livestock holdings, produce grown, land ownership, and church experience. I collected vital information by means of participant observation in homes, at church services, and at traditional ceremonies. Also, numerous informant sessions were held, both formally and informally, with local residents. Additional data were provided by outside sources such as the Navajo tribal headquarters at Window Rock, Arizona, the Bureau of Indian Affairs office in Rimrock, the Nazarene district headquarters in Phoenix, the Latter Day Saints Rimrock Ward and St. Johns (Arizona) Stake records, as well as the field notes from the extensive Harvard Rimrock projects (*see* Introduction) now stored in the library at the state's Laboratory of Anthropology in Santa Fe, New Mexico.

In order to obtain critical information regarding specialized areas of economic behavior and religious beliefs, I conducted several surveys, including a "Religious Comprehension and Preference" and an "Economic Values" questionnaire.[1] As was frequently the case in the administration of the social-census schedule, the subjects often added valuable comment in their responses to specific questions.

NOTES

1. Kendall A. Blanchard, "Religious Change and Economic Behaviour among the Rimrock Navajo" (Ph.D. dissertation, Southern Methodist University, 1971), pp. 391–96.

Acknowledgments

While in Rimrock, doing the fieldwork for this publication and getting involved in the life of the community, I developed a deep appreciation for many of its members, both Anglo and Navajo. It is to these cooperative and hospitable people, a list of whose names would be too lengthy to attempt in this section, that I am primarily indebted for the success of this work.

The idea prompting this treatise grew out of extensive correspondence with Robert Rapoport. Without his advice and counsel, I would perhaps still be floundering around in the early stages of the project.

I would like to express my gratitude to the several persons and agencies who gave me access to much valuable data in the form of records and documents. The Rimrock Ward of the Church of Jesus Christ of Latter Day Saints, the Rimrock Bureau of Indian Affairs subagency, the Church of the Nazarene North American Indian District headquarters in Phoenix, and the Navajo Tribe. In particular, I must thank Lee Correll, research director with the Tribe, for both his continued assistance and the permission to use a large portion of the material contained in chapter one.

Ben J. Wallace is to be commended for both his critical

15

insight and patience, in the role as my mentor and reader of the several drafts of this work. The following also took time from busy schedules to provide constructive suggestion and comment relative to the theoretical structure of the analysis: David Aberle, Joseph Aceves, Robert Bellah, Louis Heib, Charles Hughes, Craig Lundberg, James Peacock, John Roberts, and Evon Vogt.

Special thanks is also due George Magee for the many hours he spent combing through the manuscript with a detail that only a professional editor can achieve.

For permission to quote I thank the following: from "The Rimrock Navajo," by Clyde Kluckhohn, in their *Bulletin* 196, the Bureau of American Ethnology; from *The Protestant Ethic and the Spirit of Capitalism* (1968 edition), by Max Weber, the publisher, Charles Scribner's Sons; from *Ideological Differences and World Order,* edited by F. S. C. Northrop, in particular, the article on "The Philosophy of the Navajo Indians," by Clyde Kluckhohn, the publisher, Yale University Press.

Abbreviations

A.D.C.——Aid to Dependent Children

A.N.B.——Aid to Needy Blind

B.I.A.——Bureau of Indian Affairs

D.N.A.——*Dinébehna Naxxlna bee Agabitaxé* (People's Legal Service)

F.H.A.——Farmer's Home Administration

H.I.T.P.——Housing Improvement Training Program

L.D.S.——Church of Jesus Christ of Latter Day Saints

M.I.A.——Mutual Improvement Association (Program of the Church of Jesus Christ of Latter Day Saints)

O.A.A.——Old Age Assistance

O.N.E.O.—Office of Navajo Economic Opportunity

R.E.A.P.——Rural Environmental Assistance Program (Soil Conservation Service, U.S. Department of Agriculture)

S.U.Y.L——Sheep Units Year Long

Introduction

The first Sunday after I moved to Rimrock in the summer of 1970, I visited both of the two churches in town. I had for some time intended to study the total impact of religious change on the Navajo community and had a long list of what I considered to be relevant questions that I expected to ask my subjects. In turn, I expected to get direct, comprehensive answers. "Why do the Navajos affiliate with the Protestant mission? What is the theoretical extent of their involvement? How does the institutional environment affect Anglo-Navajo relationships? What are the economic ramifications of Navajo participation in a Protestant religious program?"

Having just moved into the area, I was still somewhat overcome by the newness of both the setting and the people. I was convinced, though, that my feelings of being lost in a novel world of unstructured data were, as was the case with my general uneasiness, simply a temporary condition; a product of mild culture shock. It would obviously be only a matter of a few days, and my new surroundings would suddenly fall into perspective; each person, place, and event fitting nicely into convenient cubbyholes of experience. At that point, actual data collection would be a routine procedure—simply raising my basic questions and filling in the blanks by picking and choosing from those readily accessible categories of information.

My optimism was short-lived. That day I spent riding the hard, wooden pews, singing hymns that I had never heard before, trying to look inconspicuous while at the same time observing everything, and asking my basic questions whenever possible exposed the naiveté of my research design.

I went to the Mormon Church first that morning. Their services were earlier than those of their cross-town rival, the Nazarene mission. There were approximately 150 persons in attendance, most of them local whites. Although some 400 area Navajos were included on Mormon membership rolls, only seven were in the congregation that particular day—two elderly women, an elderly man, and a middle-aged couple and their two small children. At one point, the younger of the two Navajo men present, Juan Begay, addressed the audience for a few moments in his native tongue for the benefit of the three older persons. With this exception, however, the entire proceedings were conducted in English—the hymns, prayers, message, and testimonies.

After the two-hour program, I was able to talk to Juan, whom I had met earlier in the week. When I asked him what I considered to be one of the simplest in my repertoire of questions—"Why did you join the Mormon Church?"—he gave me, instead of a neat, concise answer to jot down in my journal, an extensive autobiographical sketch that contained many motivational factors and rationales: a drinking problem, encouragement from mother, financial difficulties, accidental involvement in the Mormon program, and feelings of hostility toward rival institutional alternatives.

Suddenly I was faced with the frank reality that anthropological field work was more than simply fill-in-the-blanks interviewing. Even worse, I was being forced to admit that my initial feeelings of unstructuredness were not temporary. If one individual, especially one as well-educated and worldly-wise as Juan, could not give me a consistent explanation for his behavior, how could I expect a uniform rationale for a whole group? At that point I saw my problem as much more basic and ultimately more complicated than what I had earlier envisioned. I was then ready to accept the notion that in doing anthropology I would be splashing around in a sea of undefined and strange experience, fighting to keep my head above water and only hoping that in the midst of my struggles I might grasp the life-saving security of at least a fragment of statistical regularity.

Approaching the east side of town.

Still pondering the implications of my first real participant observation in Rimrock, I walked up the hill on the east edge of town to visit the Nazarene-mission services. The situation here was a complete reversal of that encountered among the Mormons. The building itself was simply a long, rectangular-block structure with a low A-frame roof, concrete floor, roughly constructed and varnished pews, with a seating capacity of about

200; this as opposed to the much more elaborate and expansive yellow-brick edifice of the Latter Day Saints.

Of the 120 persons present at the mission that day, all but the missionary, the Rev. Rockford, his wife and three children, the lady playing the organ, and myself, were Indian. Most of the women over eighteen were clothed in the traditional, colorful full skirts and velvetine blouses, with their hair done up in a knot at the back of the head. The men, outnumbered by the women more than two-to-one, were dressed in typical Navajo fashion with boots, Levis, and cowboy shirts. One of the ladies wore a rather stylish Western outfit, while two of the men sported suits and ties.

The songs, prayers, individual testimonies, and sermon were in Navajo, the missionary speaking through an interpreter. The service continued for almost four hours with no apparent order. In fact, the extensive time element appeared to be the only predictable regularity.

In general, confusion appeared to be standard fare at the Nazarene mission. During most of the afternoon's program, children ran in and out of the building, playing and yelling in the aisles with very little interference from parents. The adults, on the other hand, appeared to be only slightly more concerned with formality. Teen-agers played games in the back pews. Two women nursed small babies. Several men spent most of the afternoon sitting outside in the cabs of their pickups, at times wandering in to observe for awhile or to deliver a message. Many of the ladies, their full skirts rustling loudly, would get up unpredictably and cross to the opposite side of the sanctuary to talk with a friend. Even the Rev. Rockford himself would occasionally take temporary leave through a door behind the platform.

Often, without warning, an individual would jump to his feet and begin an oration that might last as long as forty-five minutes, as it was in the case of Charles Yazi. At eighty-five, a very prominent and respected man in the area, he talked of his own conversion to the new faith and admonished his fellow

The children of The People in Rimrock.

members on being "Christians," at times becoming extremely emotional and demonstrative. I was later told that he, as well as others, had at times used this opportunity to openly criticize the person and policies of Rev. Rockford, who, because he understood very little Navajo beyond *"yah'tee"* (polite form of greeting), would simply sit and smile or utter a hearty, "Praise the Lord!"

By the time the benediction had been pronounced, many of the original congregation had already left. Seating patterns, moods, proprieties, and activities had changed to the extent that I could barely see any relationship whatsoever between the scene then and that four hours earlier at the beginning of the service.

After I talked to the Rev. Rockford and Charles for awhile, I went back to my place, a small apartment adjacent to the Rimrock Elementary School, just down the hill from the Nazarene mission. As I sat behind my typewriter trying to put the day's events on field-note cards, I began to rise above the discouragement generated by the continuing confusion. On the one hand the possibility of seeing some meaningful pattern in that diversity of face, dress, personal style, attitude and activity seemed so distant. Yet on the other hand, the challenge gave me a new appreciation for the distinctiveness of my chosen profession.

Anthropology field work goes well beyond the post-card descriptions of the occasional tourist, the pat explanations of the deadline-oriented journalist, or the impersonal and often removed observations of the sociologist. The paradox that makes anthropology unique is its involvement that demands that it remain open to the possibility of irregularity in its search for regularity. This is both the pain and the promise of the science.

By the time I finally went to bed that night, I felt good about my stay in Rimrock and the project's future. I was excited about that complete exposure to a new cultural milieu that refuses to allow one the comforts of obvious reality and easy predictability. I was determined to keep probing until I had answered some fundamental questions. "Is there any economic significance to Navajo participation in Protestant-mission programs? If so, how does one define that significance, its causal factors, and its continuing results, as they are manifested in behavior?"

THE SETTING

The town of Rimrock itself, which the Navajos refer to as *Tl'ohchini* ("onions"), is a small village of about 280 persons, located on the northwestern border of New Mexico.[1] Founded in the 1880s by missionary-minded Mormons, the community over the years has been oriented around church activities, the majority of its citizens belonging to the Church of Jesus Christ of Latter Day Saints (L.D.S.). The village, predominantly white, lies in the northwest corner of a large stretch of land referred to

The beautiful Rimrock Valley from the west.

as the *Rimrock area*. The Rimrock business community encompasses a trading post, gas station, garage, post office, laundromat, and a small motel. The area itself extends some fourteen miles to the east of Rimrock and thirty-five miles south, comprising a total of 505 square miles, of which about fifty percent is Navajo owned. In mid-1973 there were almost 1,300 Navajos living in the Rimrock area.

For purposes of the famous Harvard Values Project, which was conducted in Rimrock during the years 1949 to 1955,[2] the area population was divided into five cultures: Navajo, Zuni, Spanish-American, Texan, and Mormon. Today there are still Zuni farmers on the western fringes of the region, but most of the Texans and the Spanish peoples are gone, having taken jobs in the larger cities to the north. In reality, the only viable groups left in the Rimrock area today are the Navajos and a general Anglo faction, the majority of whom are descendants of the original Mormon population.

Physically, the Rimrock area is marked by elevations ranging from 6,400 to 8,000 feet. Because of the altitude and the related steppe climate, temperatures tend to vary widely. For example, during the month of January in 1971 the temperatures dropped to as low as minus fifty degrees and rose to as high as sixty-two degrees above zero, all within a two-day period. While killing frosts often occur in every month except July and August, temperatures average around twenty-five in January and sixty-six in July. Precipitation brings about fifteen inches of moisture to Rimrock annually, including occasional heavy snows. The most severe snowfall recorded in Rimrock history occurred in November 1931, when thirty inches fell within two days, resulting in death for many and the loss of livestock for others. The storm had a crippling effect on the economic potential of Anglos and Navajos alike, its results felt for three or four years following the experience. Many local residents have never forgotten the tragedy.

Geographically, the area is characterized as semiarid, most of the central and southeast portions of the region covered by

A fall morning in Rimrock.

old lava beds and basaltic outcrops.[3] Other sections are marked by colored sandstone, while numerous mesas and small canyons intermittently line the rugged face of the whole area. The countryside is drained by the Zuni River, which flows southwest and empties into the Little Colorado River.

According to Paul Vestal, the soil of the area belongs to the lithosol group, soils that are "very complex, normally shallow, and subject to rapid erosion."[4] This helps to explain much of the eroded land and the many large arroyos, although in the case of the latter, overgrazing, cultivation, and road construction must also bear part of the blame.

Vegetation in the Rimrock area falls into two broad categories relative to altitude. The higher elevations are marked by a landscape of coniferous trees—mainly yellow pine—with short grasses. The lower region, the juniper-pinyon zone, is characterized by pinyon pine, one-seed juniper, Rocky Mountain juniper, and short grasses with many shrubs: sage brush, mountain mahogany, and Apache plume. In some of the valleys one finds Douglas fiir and Engelmann spruce, while along the waterways are occasional cottonwood and willow trees.

The most common animal wildlife in the area are the rabbits, both jack and cottontail. While they have long been hunted by whites and Navajos alike for either sport or food, they continue to flourish. One local resident tells of an evening a few years ago when he and two friends went "spot-lighting" (that is, using a bright spot-light to sight and blind the animals) and shot seventy-nine of the small animals in less than four hours.

When Landgraf reported his findings relative to the situation around 1940,[5] he noted that the prairie dog population had fallen off due to hunting by the Navajos and federal rodent-control measures. However, recently more and more colonies of these small mammals have been springing up and are continuing to menace Navajo farmers in the area.

Other animals in the region include squirrel, field mice, rats, gophers, coyotes, foxes, and lately, a great host of skunks. Hunters shot quite a few deer in the country around Rimrock in 1972, and while bobcats and mountain lions were reported in 1970, no one has seen black bears, wolves, or mountain sheep since around 1960.

The predominant reptile in the area is the horned toad, although many rattlesnakes were seen and killed during 1972. The pinyon jay dominates the bird population. Also common are the spurred towhees, swallows, swifts, and sparrows. Occasionally, owls, woodpeckers, and blackbirds have been observed. During the few years previous to 1972, an increasing number of crows had been flourishing. Game birds, such as quail and grouse, were once more frequently encountered than they have been in recent periods, and due to low water levels previous to the spring of 1973, very few ducks have come into the Rimrock area during the winter months in recent years.

ANTHROPOLOGISTS AND RIMROCK

In order to appreciate any theoretical work growing out of the Rimrock situation, it is important to recognize the area's scholarly heritage. If it were possible to calculate the number of hours spent by anthropologists doing field work in the Rimrock area in relation to either geographical size or population, it could probably be demonstrated that Rimrock residents, especially the Indians, are the most studied people in the world. A good percentage of the published material on the Navajos has come out of Rimrock. In fact, in many cases, students with a limited book knowledge of *the* Navajos are actually only familiar with the *Rimrock* Navajos.

Anthropological interest in Rimrock dates back to 1923 when Clyde Kluckhohn came to the village to recuperate from a severe case of tuberculosis.[6] In the summers from 1926 to 1930 the anthropologist spent many days in Rimrock working with the Navajos. Many of the old-timers in Rimrock still have their Clyde Kluckhohn stories. An elderly Anglo-Mormon, Aaron Cox, worked with the young anthropologist in those early days and recalls the reaction of the community that first summer :

> I'll never forget when he first come to town. Nobody really knew quite what to make of him. He wore them Levis with some old boots and a cowboy hat. I guess in a way we was all kind of scared of him. . . . He'd go around and he'd pay the Navvies fifty cents an hour to sit down and talk to him. We really didn't know what he was doing, . . . but he turned out to be a pretty nice feller.

Between 1932 and 1934, while teaching at the University of New Mexico, Kluckhohn made many trips to Rimrock. Then in 1936—after completing work toward his doctorate at Harvard—he planned, under the direction of Edward Sapir and John Dollard, an extended study of Navajo children and the socialization process.

Rimrock was selected as the locale for several reasons : some knowledge had been accumulated and easy entreé existed. The Rimrock Navajo had led an isolated, rural life in competition with their English- and Spanish-speaking neighbors. Prior to May 1940, there was no sustained supervision from the Indian Service. The first government school in the area was built in 1943. Contact with missionaries hardly began until 1944. Finally, the Rimrock Navajo were geographically isolated from other Navajo groups. There was no question as to where the social system began or ended.[7]

Simultaneous with this research, a broader program of ethnographic investigation evolved, and there soon developed the idea "that the following of a small community and its culture through time was a needed experiment in anthropology."[8]

During the year 1940, Kluckhohn, in working out this more inclusive project with the help of Alexander and Dorothea Leighton, decided that in addition to telescoping the time element, the anthropologist should also attempt to capitalize on *all* available data as seen from a collection of disciplinary perspectives. Thus the methods of "multiple observation" and "multiple approaches" were applied to the Rimrock project. From that year until the termination of the project, the research remained "consistently collaborative and cumulative."[9]

Over the next few years a host of field workers swarmed the Rimrock area. The first report of the Rimrock project lists thirty-two workers representing a wide range of academic disciplines. Some of the more prominent figures included : David Aberle, John Adair, Bert Kaplan, John Landgraf, John Roberts, James Spuhler, Harry Tschopik, Paul Vestal, and Evon Vogt, among others. Besides professional anthropologists and graduate students, participants included medical doctors, psychologists, a botanist, and several psychiatrists.[10]

The "Comparative Study of Values in Five Cultures Project," under the direction of the Laboratory of Social Relations at Harvard, grew out of the older Rimrock project and was designed during the years 1948 and 1949. The new study was formally initiated in June 1949.[11] The Rimrock area was chosen not only because of the great volumes of accumulated background work, but also for the availability of the "five contrasting cultures for comparative study."[12]

Its field headquarters in Rimrock and with John Roberts as coordinator and Evon Vogt as deputy director, the Values Project was not actually terminated until 1955, although most of the field work was completed by 1953. During the research years in Rimrock, some thirty-seven scholars from anthropology, sociology, psychology, political science, philosophy, history, and geography were represented in the field, and the experiences produced many books, dissertations, articles, and papers.[13]

It was during the period around 1950 when the influx of researchers had its greatest impact on the Rimrock community. One resident calls this period "the years of the 'ologists.' " With the heaviest concentration in the summer time, each year the town of Rimrock was besieged with a variety of scholars and students; some lived in tents or rented rooms from the Mormon citizens, while others lived in hogans with the Navajos. Patronizing local business establishments and talking to and questioning every man, woman, and child in the area, the visitors left weighty impressions and in many cases established lasting relationships with local inhabitants.

From the first phases of the project in the early forties, the field notes of the workers were collected and processed by data analysts in the Peabody Museum at Harvard. The materials were dittoed, and individual notes cross-filed by researchers, informant names, and subject area, in accordance with the system of Murdock's Human Relations Area Files. The Rimrock files, with their drawer after drawer of duplicated field notes on five-by-eight-inch pieces of paper, were moved to the library at the Laboratory of Anthropology in Santa Fe in March of 1968.

Although the Values Project was terminated some fifteen years ago, the Rimrock case is anything but closed. Field work under the direction of the Harvard program has long been discontinued, but there is still an acting director, and much of the unpublished material is still being processed. Also, since the days of the project, a number of graduate students from Harvard, Cornell, Columbia, and other schools have spent summer months in the Rimrock area working on specific anthropological problems.

One local Navajo, Chavez Begay, a well-known ceremonial practitioner, began working with Kluckhohn back in the early thirties. He and his family have hosted so many field workers that they once built a special hogan "for the anthropologists." One of Chavez's older boys once told me that he had been around so many anthropologists in the past that he already knew the rules of the game, and in fact had ambitions of getting into the profession. When I asked him directly what anthropologists were, he replied, "They're people that drive big cars and have lots of cigarettes."

Because of the intensity of the research conducted in Rimrock over the past forty years, the oft-expressed opinion is that, in terms of anthropological value, it has been overworked. Perhaps for those interested in traditional ethnographic data, the situation might limit opportunities for novelty. However, where problems of change and economic development are involved, such as in my case, such a context is ideal. The many publications, the Rimrock files, and the experience of many professional anthropologists make the Rimrock area a virtual laboratory for the study of culture change.

The flurry of anthropological activity in Rimrock around 1950 produced volumes of material. Of all the books, articles, papers, and field notes, the most important study coming out of this period for my purpose was Rapoport's comprehensive and well-known work on religious change, "Changing Navajo Religious Values."[14] In this Peabody Museum Paper that grew out of a dissertation, the author looks at the determinants underlying Navajo affiliation with the several available religious alternatives in the area in terms of basic personality needs.

THEORETICAL FRAMEWORK

The religious situation among the Rimrock Navajos today
is characterized by the presence of three fairly distinct groups:
Mormon, Nazarene, and traditional. Rimrock was settled originally by evangelizing Latter Day Saints, and technically there
have been Mormon Navajos in the area since the early 1870s.
In fact, according to local church records, "by October of
1877, thirty-four Navajos had been baptized." [15] However, it
was not until after World War II that a concerted effort was
made by the Rimrockites to convert large segments of the area
Navajo population.

The Church of the Nazarene, a small evangelical holiness
group, first sent missionaries into the Rimrock area in 1944.
Despite early difficulties, by the first years of the fifties the
Nazarenes had become a prominent force in the Indian
community.

Traditional is the term I have chosen to identify those
Navajos in the Rimrock area who have as yet been relatively
unaffected by any outside religious group and as such still cling
to the ideological principles characterizing "the old way"
(*'aal'kidaa'yáá k'ehgo*).

Due to the size of the area population, I was forced to
focus primarily on a representative sample of thirty-four family
groups, by which I mean a collection of related individuals,
often involving as many as four generations, living together in
the same immediate area, sharing meals and to a certain extent
responsibilities, and including those children who upon reaching
maturity have moved away. [16] Because there was a fairly regular
pattern to intrafamilial religious sympathies, I was able to cat-
egorize these groups according to religious affiliation as defined
above. Again, in order to qualify as either Mormon or Nazarene,
a family group must have demonstrated by long-term participation, their commitment to a particular program. Ultimately,
then, the total sample involved over forty per cent of the Navajos
in the area (*see* Table 1). [17]

However, because most of my statistical comparisons involved only those individuals whom I designated as economically responsible and still residing in the Rimrock area, my actual working sample was considerably smaller, but still sign-

Table 1

Total sample

	Family Groups	First Generation	Second Generation	Third Generation	Total Persons
Traditional	(17)	28	119	176	323
Mormon	(4)	8	46	54	108
Nazarene	(13)	19	77	94	190
Total	(34)	55	242	324	621

nificantly representative (*see* Table 2). By "economic responsibility" I mean the condition whereby one is at least eighteen years of age, of sound mind and body, and no longer in public school.

Table 2

Working sample

	Family Groups	First Generation	Second Generation	Third Generation	Total Persons
Traditional	(17)	28	76	18	122
Mormon	(4)	8	30	2	40
Nazarene	(13)	19	48	4	71
Total	(34)	55	154	24	233

From a general perspective, the major theoretical issue raised in this study concerns the nature of the relationship between religious belief and economic behavior. While most of his substantive theory has been discounted, no one yet has displaced Max Weber and his historical role of having most adequately raised the important questions in his classic work, *The Protestant Ethic and the Spirit of Capitalism.*[18] Therefore, one can not afford to ignore him in attempting to treat the broad impact of Protestantism.[19]

In an even more localized context than that explored by Clifford Geertz in Indonesia, the basic thrust here is to focus the Weber problem on a limited situation as opposed to "the grand overall approach which Weber used, the correlation of social structures and religious systems for whole civilizations over the entire course of their history."[20] No attempt is being made to either prove or disprove any of Weber's theoretical propositions in the analysis. In harmony with the manner in which the problem was originally stated:

> we only wish to ascertain whether and to what extent religious forces have taken part in the qualitative formation and the quantitative expansion of that spirit [the spirit of capitalism] over the world.[21]

In conjunction with an effort to raise the Protestant-ethic question in a limited situation, it has become necessary to qualify the original formulation of the problem. In the first place, it would be very difficult to talk in terms of an emerging industrial order among the Rimrock Navajos. Also, broad patterns of entrepreneurship reflecting Weber's worldwide spirit of capitalism are locally nonexistent. Therefore, this analysis will approach the theoretical problem of the interrelationship of ideological and economic aspects of culture at a microeconomic level. Instead of looking for major industrial developments and capitalistic enterprises, this investigation will orient itself toward less spectacular, individual experience that can be characterized in terms of an idealized behavioral continuum ranging from economic traditionalism to economic rationalism. Economic rationalism is that attitude characterizing the pursuit of typically

Western, capitalistic-economic goals, while economic traditionalism is the mood defining the various economic activities
associated with precontact Navajo society.

In considering the applicative value of Weber's thesis at
the microeconomic level, further clarification is in order. The
tendency here will be to deemphasize causal implications and
look rather to what Eisenstadt has recently labeled "the internal
transformative capacities of Protestantism":

> By transformation capacity is meant the capacity to legitimize,
> in religious or ideological terms the development of new motiva-
> tions, activities, and institutions which were not encompassed
> by their original impulses and views.[22]

Since Weber, the emphasis in looking at the economic
impact of the Protestant church has generally been on the
dogmatic roots of its ethic. The eminent sociologist himself
directed primary attention to

> the influence of those psychological sanctions which, originating
> in religious belief and the practice of religion, gave a direction
> to practical conduct and held the individual to it. Now these
> sanctions were to a large extent derived from the peculiarities
> of the religious ideas behind them. The men of that day were
> occupied with abstract dogma to an extent which itself can
> only be understood when we perceive the connection of these
> dogmas with practical religious instinct.[23]

Likewise, there has been a tendency for both sociologists and
anthropologists to overlook the formative influence of the institutional life of Protestantism in its impact on the other phases of
society. Therefore, for purposes of this investigation, I am suggesting that Eisenstadt's transformative-capacities concept can
be more productive if it is understood in terms of two logical
subcomponents that I have labeled *theological-ethical capacities*
and *institutional capacities*.

Inherent in the first subdivision are the theoretical aspects of
the traditional Protestant-ethic problem. It was at this level, for
example, that Weber outlined the implications for economic

behavior latent in the Calvinistic notion of predestination. Here also are contained the ideological roots of those psychological sanctions and motivations related to other behavioral patterns. In this sense the theological-ethical capacities are the more purely religious functions of the transformative duality.

On the other hand, the institutional capacities are those processes operative at a more practical, secular level. Here, I am arguing, one can isolate some of the directly formative influences of the church's role in a particular society. In this area are encountered the function of the fellowship, the distribution and exchange of services inherent in the mission program, and the effect of the personal advice and direction of the missionaries.

In scrutinizing this idealized dichotomy—theological-ethical capacities on the one hand versus the institutional capacities on the other—one can legitimately characterize the latter as *secular* as opposed to *religious* in their actual manifestations; *direct* as opposed to *indirect*; *explicit* as opposed to *implicit*; *practical* as opposed to *theoretical*.

Figure 1

The role of transformative capacities in economic change

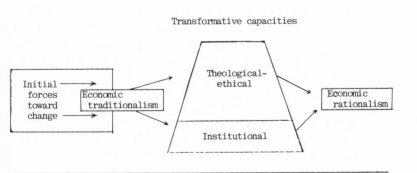

Transformative capacities

Theological-ethical

Institutional

Initial forces toward change

Economic traditionalism

Economic rationalism

This model, defined in terms of its dualistic oppositions, gives one more effective analytic leverage with which to consider the total significance of the appearance of Protestantism on the Navajo scene in Rimrock.

My initial hypothesis is simply that, in terms of the indicators selected for this study, the churched Navajos in Rimrock tend to do better economically than do the nonchurched. In other words, the churched people tend to act more economically rational than do the nonchurched, in the sense that this notion has been previously defined; making more money, having better jobs, getting more education and special training, exhibiting greater geographical mobility, and performing more efficiently on the job. Recognizing the fact that ecological factors in the Rimrock area play a limiting role where economic decisions are involved, it is further proposed that the churched Navajos are adapting better to the new demands of wage labor.

The most dramatic differentials in the statistical portrayal of economic behavior occur when results for women are isolated and compared, and also when second-generation figures are analyzed. Navajo women, as Hughes has earlier noted, are much more active participants in the Christian missions than the men.[24] Second-generation family members in each of the religious groups, on the other hand, have had longer periods of time during which to be exposed to the various influences of the Protestant institution. In terms of what is known about the individual Rimrock Navajo, his situation some twenty years ago, and the events occurring since then, it is observed that, from a comparative perspective, first-generation sample people have altered their economic life-styles only slightly. Thus, the differentials of significance at this level are much the same as those that existed two decades ago.

In light of these observations, it seems obvious that the initial role of the Protestant ethic can not be demonstrated as causative, acting at best in terms of its transformative capacities as an ideological instrument of legitimization. However, with the more radical changes and comparative distinctions that occur at the second-generation level, the possibility of a formative role for the missions' influences becomes more realistic. This is especially evident in light of individual situations where critical historical information concerning behavior changes and their causes is available. With this data as given, then, I am suggesting that in the process of economic change there are situations where transformative capacities do more than legitimize previously altered patterns of behavior, but actually give additional meaning to and accelerate the newly selected styles.

This accelerative-formative process toward greater economic rationalism is predicated on many observable characteristics in the institutional life of the church. For example, extended participation in mission activities accentuates the function of the fellowship in breaking down old and creating new social alignments. It also serves to broaden world views beyond the context of traditional commitments. Again, the admonitions of the missionaries in practical areas such as special training, economic responsibility or investment, coupled with educational and travel opportunties, provide additional change incentives and motivations.

From the theological-ethical perspective, formative influences are less obvious. While ethical proscriptions, such as the bans against drinking, smoking, and gambling, have direct economic implications, the role of the more mystical theological issues is very obscure. Rimrock-Navajo Christians are not motivated by abstract theological discussion to the same extent that Weber's sixteenth- and seventeenth-century Calvinists supposedly were. They also do not internalize basic Christian concepts in the same way as do their Anglo counterparts, and their church experience is relatively deficient in theological and historical depth. From the other side of the relationship here, in the messages of both the Mormon and the Nazarene missionaries, the notions of spiritual well-being and other-worldly rewards are very rarely, if ever, correlated with this-worldly success. Work has never been stressed purely for work's sake, nor has there been any explicit attempts made to ground economic change in theological propositions. Therefore, the evidence suggests that, in the sense in which the idea was employed by Weber, the Protestant ethic plays a comparatively minor role in both its legitimizing and formative effects on the economic styles of Rimrock-Navajo Christians. Even in the area of ethical proscriptions, the Navajos tend to rely on unique, practical rationales that ultimately bypass theological or biblical authority, typical of a tendency inherent in traditional Navajo thought-ways.

In terms of the practical value of an investigation into the total impact of religious change, Eisenstadt indicates that

> the extent to which secular-ideological movements are successful may also greatly depend on the degree to which they are able to develop from within themselves transformative orientations, on different levels of individual behaviour, and new roles and organizational frameworks similar to those of religious movements.[25]

If this is the case, then it is very likely that the mechanics of the institutional capacities will afford more immediate insight and greater applicability to secular problems than do the situational functioning of theoretical-ethical propositions in Rimrock.

Some writers have chosen to portray the experience of the individual Navajo's conversion to any of the several forms of Christianity as a radical ideological change.[26] In opposition to this picture, I am also arguing that, while the change is certainly more than incidental, it is an event relatively consistent with preexistent patterns. This is *true,* but not necessarily because of the nature of the Christian message. Rather it is a result of the adaptability and discriminatory insight of the Navajos in the change process.[27] This talent, while it mollifies the psychological effects of new religious experience, works to the detriment of the Protestant ethic's economic possibilities by sorting out and reinterpreting those aspects of foreign theology that are too radically opposed to fundamental elements within existing value systems and thought patterns.

In essence, then, the hypothesis that this work substantiates is that the primary role of the Protestant church among the Rimrock Navajos in economic change is simply one of presenting new options, legitimizing altered behavior patterns, and in some cases accelerating the quantitative results of these changes, all by means of its transformative results. Because of the nature of the Rimrock situation and the various problems that arise in conjunction with the theoretical question of how religious and economic behavior are related, it is likewise contended that the most important operations performed by the transformative capacities of the church emanate from the institutional aspects of the dichotomy. On the other hand, because the theological-ethical capacities appear to be of limited causal or explanatory value in the area of Rimrock-Navajo economic behavioral changes, I conclude that the Protestant-ethic concept is relatively meaningless in the attempt to understand this situation.

NOTES

1. *Tl'ohchini* means "the place of the onions" and is used by the Navajos to refer to Rimrock because of a particular strong-smelling plant that is common in the area directly around the town itself.

2. For a complete list of the publications coming out of the Values Project, *see* the Appendix of *People of Rimrock,* eds. Evon Z. Vogt and Ethel M. Albert (Cambridge, Massachusetts: Harvard University Press, 1967).

3. John L. Landgraf, "Land-use in the Rimrock Area of New Mexico," *Peabody Museum Papers* 42, no. 1 (1954):8–25.

4. Paul A. Vestal, "Ethnobotany of the Rimrock Navajo," *Peabody Museum Papers* 40, no. 4 (1952): 3.

5. Landgraf, p. 23.

6. *See* Clyde Kluckhohn, *To the Foot of the Rainbow* (New York: Century, 1927).

7. Clyde Kluckhohn, "The Rimrock Project," in Alexander H. Leighton and Dorothea C. Leighton, "Gregario, the Hand-trembler," *Peabody Museum Papers* 40, no. 1 (1949):50.

8. Ibid.

9. Ibid., p. 6.

10. Alexander H. Leighton and Dorothea C. Leighton, "Gregario, the Hand-trembler," *Peabody Museum Papers* 40, no. 1 (1949):7–9.

11. Evon Z. Vogt and Ethel M. Albert, "The Comparative Study of Value in Five Cultures Project," in *People of Rimrock,* eds. Vogt and Albert (Cambridge, Massachusetts: Harvard University Press, 1967), p. 6.

12. Ibid., p.7.

13. *See* note 2 above; ibid., p. 8.

14. Robert N. Rapoport, "Changing Navajo Religious Values," *Peabody Museum Papers* 40, no. 1 (1949):50.

15. Irving Telling, "History of Rimrock, New Mexico" (Unpublished manuscript, Harvard University, 1939), p. 2.

16. The concept is similar to Clyde Kluckhohn's definition of "unit," except that it is not limited to continued residence in the same kin environment. In other words, if a child marries and moves away from his family of orientation, he is still considered a member of that original family group; *see* Clyde Kluckhohn, "The Rimrock Navajo," *Bureau of American Ethnology Bulletin* 196 (1966): 366.

17. For a more detailed description of the sampling procedure *see* Blanchard, "Religious Change," pp. 15–18.

18. Max Weber, *The Protestant Ethic and the Spirit of Capitalism,* trans. Talcott Parsons, 1968 edition (New York: Scribner's, 1904).

19. While Mormons deny their historical and theological status as Protestants, there is no way to avoid the fact that the movement was born out of the turmoil of eighteenth-century Protestant revivalism. In many areas directly reflecting theological consequences of this birth, the "this-worldly-success" ideology of Mormonism is perhaps more closely related to Weber's Protestant-ethic ideal type than even that of Reformation Calvinism. Every L.D.S. sermon and testimony in the typical white ward is replete with references to the inherent value of hard work, self-discipline, and the dollar.

20. Clifford Geertz, "Religious Belief and Economic Behaviour in a Central Javanese Town," in *The Protestant Ethic and Modernization,* ed. S. N. Eisenstadt (New York: Basic Books, 1968), p. 309.

21. Weber, p. 91.

22. S. N. Eisenstadt, "The Protestant-ethic Thesis in an Analytical and Comparative Framework," in *The Protestant Ethic and Modernization,* ed. S. N. Eisenstadt (New York: Basic Books, 1968), p. 8.

23. Weber, pp. 97–98.

24. Charles E. Hughes, "The Navajo Woman and Nazarene Christianity" (Honors thesis, Harvard University, 1951), p. 1.

25. Eisenstadt, p. 37.

26. *See,* for example, Gladys Reichard, "The Navajo and Christianity," *American Anthropologist* 51 (1949):66–71; Hughes.

27. John Adair and Evon Z. Vogt, "Navajo and Zuni Veterans: A Study in Contrasting Modes of Culture Change," *American Anthropologist* 51 (1949):547–61.

THE ECONOMICS
OF SAINTHOOD

I

The People, Past and Present

The Navajos' designation of themselves as *Diné (The People)* is a manifestation of the fierce pride that has helped them survive many dramatic setbacks and traumatic economic changes in their relatively short history in the Southwest. Archaeologists are almost uniformly convinced that the Navajos have been in that part of the country for less than 500 years. During that time they have radically changed their basic subsistence patterns three times: from hunting and gathering to farming; from farming to raising sheep and raiding; and from that to a direct involvement in the Western wage economy. They have been hunted, enslaved, shot, and imprisoned, but they have flourished in the midst of their adversity and today are the largest of American Indian groups, with a population of over 130,000 and a strong sense of cultural integrity and self-determination.

The Rimrock Navajos, like their fellow tribesmen on the Reservation, are products of the same tumultuous history and manifest the same inner strength. Although as late as 1950, one anthropologist concluded that the Rimrock Navajos "have never constituted a unified and tightly knit community," many things have taken place since that time to give new meaning and purpose to their life together.[1] The trend of this growing sense of community and political unity provides a natural framework for the analysis of Rimrock-Navajo history and contemporary cultural patterns in terms of the following four phases:

1) Settlement and Stabilization (circa 1869–1919);
2) Allotment (1920–1939);
3) Definition (1940–1969);
4) A New Sense of Community (1970– ?).

HISTORY

The unresolved question regarding the history of the Navajos in the Rimrock area is whether or not there were any of The People settled there prior to the Navajos' return from Fort Sumner captivity in 1868, or during the years immediately following. To date, most of the evidence suggests that they had been in the region for a long time before their tragic imprisonment.

Worcester suggested that it was a group of Navajos who helped the Zunis defend themselves against Coronado in 1540.[2] If this was the case, it is quite likely that the Navajos were familiar with the Rimrock area some twenty miles to the east. Additional support for this notion that the Navajos were in the general vicinity of Rimrock as early as the sixteenth century is contained in the journal of the Spanish explorer Antonio de Espejo.[3] During his expedition into New Mexico (1582–1583) he and his party encountered the Querechos or Corechos, generally conceded to have been Navajos, near the province of Acoma, slightly northeast of the Rimrock area.

Tree-ring dates from the area provide another type of evidence lending credibility to the pre-Fort Sumner Rimrock-

Navajo idea. By analyzing the concentric rings in cross sections of hewn, yet preserved trees, archaeologists are able to determine with reasonable accuracy when particular logs had been harvested. On the basis of this method, forty-nine timbers from hogans, sweathouses, and sheep corrals located on Navajo archaeological sites in the general vicinity of Rimrock have been studied. These logs yielded dates ranging from 1543 to 1925, suggesting that Navajos were established in the area throughout the period—from as early as the late 1500s until they were taken to Fort Sumner.[4]

It appears that the territory occupied by the Navajos—certainly by the early years of the eighteenth century—extended into at least portions of the Rimrock area. Kluckhohn quotes from a letter written by Governor Francisco Guervo Valdez (Santa Fe, 18 August 1706) in which El Morro (located some twelve miles east of Rimrock) is specifically named as living within "the extensive province of Navajo."[5] Also, one of the earliest known maps of Navajo country (1778–1779) falls short by only a few miles of including the northern edges of the Rimrock territory.[6]

While there is a possibility that Indians in this area during the eighteenth and nineteenth centuries were actually Apache, the case for their being Navajo is much more substantial. Documentary evidence, such as the Spanish-Navajo treaty of 1819 and the reports of travelers and military men, argues strongly in favor of the suggestion that there were Navajos in the Rimrock area at least by the early 1800s. Older Indians in the region have supported this by their claims that in the 1840s a group of them was driven out of the Crownpoint area to the north by warring Utes, and were forced to take up residence across the Zuni Mountains to the south in the vicinity of Rimrock. According to this report, there were several Navajo families farming and hunting in the present Rimrock Reservoir region during the pre-Fort Sumner period, up until 1864. Bidaga, one of the great leaders of the Rimrock Navajo, once contended:

I was born in Rimrock before the Navajo went to Fort Sumner. The grand parents and great grand parents of the Navajos who lived in Rimrock now lived there long before going to Fort Sumner. The Navajos have lived in Rimrock for six generations. My parents told me about the trip to Fort Sumner, for I was a little baby.

My parents and the ancestors of the Rimrock people were young folks when they came back from Fort Sumner. They returned to the very place they left, the valley of Rimrock.

Because our parents and our grand parents were raised and died there, we feel about this land as though it were our mother and father. It is the only place for us to live. The place where my family and the other Navajo lived was near the head of the present Rimrock Lake. There are still the remains of our old hogans around the lake.[7]

Rimrock lake.

This and other similar claims are substantiated by personal history sheets from the Zuni Hospital clinical records, birth and death certifications, and Indian-scout pension records. These sources indicate that at least forty-one Navajos were born in the Rimrock area during the period between 1838 and 1868.[8]

While the majority of the evidence suggests that the Navajos were permanently settled in the Rimrock area before the Fort Sumner tragedy, the white residents of the village prefer to see the Indian presence in the region prior to this event as only sporadic and temporary. As one older member of the Mormon community has argued:

> The Navajos never settled permanently in the Rimrock area prior to Fort Sumner. They made some extended trips into the area for hunting and raiding, but they didn't really settle down and herd sheep and grow corn, at least like they did in other areas, until later.

Despite Anglo protestations to the contrary, the idea that there was a pre-Fort Sumner Navajo band in the Rimrock area appears to be a historical reality. Illustrating how convincing this argument has become in recent years, the Indian Claims Commission in June 1970 officially recognized Navajo aboriginial territory prior to 1868 as having included the Rimrock area.[9]

Phase 1: Settlement and Stabilization (circa 1869–1919)

Regardless of how one resolves the question of a pre-Fort Sumner Rimrock-Navajo group, the history of today's community perhaps can be more adequately treated if the post-captivity period is employed as a base. Following their release from Fort Sumner in June of 1868, two Navajo family groups, or *outfits,* as anthropologists have labeled them, resettled in the Rimrock area. Though both groups have become identified by their respective male leaders, Old Man Cojo and Many Beads, in neither case were these family heads the eldest; local residents have chosen this means merely to identify the outfits. Some dispute remains as to which group settled first, and as to whether they had lived there prior to Fort Sumner. In any case, by the early 1870s there were approximately twenty-five Navajos living just to the north of the present site of Rimrock.[10]

Cultural styles of these early residents, similar to those of their tribesmen who returned to the reservation area itself, were rooted in traditional patterns. The oldest economic activity of significance to the Rimrock Navajos was that of hunting and gathering. Various game animals, such as deer and rabbits, were hunted and eaten; plants were collected for ritual, medicinal, and food purposes; and wood was gathered for fuel and dwelling construction. During these early years of Navajo experience in the Rimrock area, a few crops were also cultivated, in particular, corn, beans, and squash. They herded small flocks of sheep, and each family owned several horses that they used for both livelihood and pleasure. Sheep also were important as a source of meat and wool, the latter being used in weaving and in the manufacture of many important household items.

Herding the sheep is everyone's responsibility.

The Rimrock-Navajo family essentially was matrilineal and the postmarital pattern tended toward matrilocality, meaning that kinship was reckoned through the female genealogy, and newly married couples took up residence in the general area of the wife's family. Clan membership was a very important consideration, especially in marriage. In selecting a mate, a person avoided, in order of importance, members of his father's clan, members of his father's linked-clan group, and any individual whose father was a member of his own father's clan. The most important clans among the Rimrock Navajos in these early days were the Meadow (*Haltsooidine'é*), Bitter Water (*Todích'íi'nii*), and Alkaline Water (*Todik'oonzhii*) groups.

During this early period each household had a small area of land, or home plot, that contained several adjoining fields, one or more hogans—usually "made of logs laid in saddle-notched fashion to form a hexagonal or octagonal dome-shaped structure, surmounted by an open smokehole and roofed and floored with earth . . ."—a *chaha'oh* (a temporary shade or shelter constructed of poles and branches), corral, and small sweathouse.[11]

The first few years of resettlement after 1869 brought the Navajos into direct contact with their old enemies, the Spanish-Americans, several groups of whom moved into the area during this period. Despite basic distrust and misgivings on both sides of the encounter, sufficient space was available at this time to avoid large-scale land disputes.

From these Spanish-Americans the Navajos obtained sheep to increase their small herds, learned better methods of animal husbandry, and relations between the two groups tended to stabilize around a mutual respect. While interaction was limited, open hostilities actually were nonexistent.

In the late 1870s, Mormons began to move into the Rimrock area, an event that marked the initiation of a long era of land disputes. Under pressures of persecution and expansion, the Latter Day Saints began to settle in various parts of northern Arizona and New Mexico with instructions to "convert the

Lamanites" (the *Book of Mormon* name for all North American Indians) and "tame the land." Despite their religious zeal and enthusiasm for the well-being of the Indians, in most confrontations between missionary and prospective convert, the latter come away the obvious loser, and the experience had a memorable impact on Navajo attitudes.

The first event drastically affecting Navajo land rights in the area occurred in 1866. That year the U.S. Congress passed the Enabling Act under which the railroads were granted forty miles—later extended to fifty—of land on either side of its tracks in certain parts of the United States, including New Mexico. By this act the best sections of land in the northern part of the Rimrock area thus became privately owned property. Matters were further complicated by the Treaty of 1 June 1868, negotiated between the government and the Navajos. The boundaries of the new reservation were established by that treaty. Any who took up residence on public or private land beyond reservation confines forfeited all rights and privileges conferred by the treaty. In reality, the Rimrock Navajos were therefore left with no legal property rights, and most often were treated simply as squatters. White settlers coming into Rimrock or other areas bordering the newly created reservation could thus lay claim to lands occupied by Navajos.

When Mormons first moved into the Rimrock area, they made it known that they came in search of land. Ignoring claims of Navajos living in the region, the Saints settled on the choice sections near the spring north of present-day Rimrock.

During the 1880s lands were surveyed for homesteading, and efforts were made to set up boundaries and establish property claims in areas of New Mexico, of which Rimrock is a part. The railroad, as well as other private and public interests, soon had their land holdings well defined. The whole procedure was very confusing and frustrating to the Rimrock Navajos, and as homesteaders filed for the more desirable plots, the Indians were forced onto the unproductive sections in the barren regions southeast of Rimrock.

Because of misunderstanding and the fact that existing laws left non-reservation Indians with few rights and little bargaining leverage in land disputes, the Mormon tactics appeared ruthless and unjust to the Navajos. As the Saints obtained legal rights to the more fertile lands near the spring, the Navajos were further pressured into collecting their belongings and moving.

It was not until the 1920s, when the Rimrock Navajos began to take advantage of opportunities afforded by the Allotment Act of 1887, that they obtained legally defensible rights to lands they were occupying. On the other hand, because of the inferior quality of the sections eventually settled by the dispossessed Navajos, these lands were not coveted by their non-Indian neighbors, and during the latter years of this first phase, there were only a few land disputes between Anglos and Navajos.

Despite land problems and forced resettlement, after 1875 the Navajo population around Rimrock increased rapidly. By 1890, as a result of immigration and an impressive birth rate, there were eleven families totaling some seventy individuals comprising the Rimrock-Navajo community.[12]

Perhaps the most well-known early Navajo settler in the Rimrock area was Many Beads. Informally recognized as leader of the Rimrock Navajos for many years, Many Beads's background was that of a courageous warrior. He was a very dynamic, forceful individual, and often referred to himself as, "Number One." According to local tradition, he once attempted to take a Rimrock-Mormon woman for his third wife. Despite his gallantry and persistance, the effort eventually failed. Many Beads, also remembered by the whites as a great leader, was reportedly the first important Mormon convert among the Rimrock Navajos. As one Mormon recalled:

He (Many Beads) used to get the people together at the chicken pulls and tell them to stay away from whiskey and look after their stock. He would hold up his arms (gesture of embracing) and say, "Hold on to it like that." They really minded him.[13]

Two other prominent Navajos, both of whom settled in the Rimrock area during the latter part of the nineteenth century, were Jake Carisozo and Salao Leon. These two men enlisted as scouts for the U.S. Army, and served during the campaigns of 1880 against Geronimo and the Apaches. Salao, born in the area of the San Juan River, had lived with the Utes for several years as a boy. After his father was killed by Mexicans, he moved to the Zuni area. Following his release from Fort Sumner in 1868, he took an Apache wife, and several years afterward moved into the Rimrock area.

In many ways, Jake Carisozo was even more colorful than Salao. Like the latter, he had lived a rather mobile life, married an Apache woman, and settled in the Rimrock area in the 1880s. Because of an injury suffered in the Apache wars, Jake lost the use of his right arm. For this reason, he was known by other members of the community as, "Crippled Arm." Despite this infirmity, and later his blindness, Jake was surprisingly active up until the time of his death in 1942.

One of the wealthiest Navajos in the history of the Rimrock area, Old Man Antonio, moved into the region during the late 1880s. According to local sources, just prior to the stock-reduction program of the 1930s, Antonio had a herd of over 7,000 sheep. He was killed in a tragic car accident in 1960.

Bidaga, son of Many Beads, is recognized by many as the most outstanding Navajo in Rimrock history. So named because of his red moustache, Bidaga was a prominent ceremonial practitioner, a noted thinker, and an astute politician. Less colorful and dynamic than his father, Bidaga established his reputation by working incessantly for the well-being of the Rimrock Navajos until the time of his death in 1956.

Besides Old Man Cojo and Many Beads noted above, other prominent Navajos who settled early in the Rimrock area included No Hat, Big Red Eye, Jose Naton, Loin Cloth and Tall Loin Cloth, and Frank Eraicho. Generally, most Rimrock Navajos today point to one or more of these men as their direct ancestors, who rightfully deserve the title, "Founding Fathers."

After 1890, no new families joined the Rimrock-Navajo population. All immigration since that time has been a direct result of marriage between the Rimrock and Eastern or other Navajo groups. Generally this has been balanced by emigration stemming from the normal reciprocity of marriage arrangements.

This first phase of Navajo history in the Rimrock area was characterized by settlement, initial contacts with Mormon Anglos, land disputes, resettlement, and a general attitude of frustration and defeat. While the Navajos faced many problems in their attempt to wrest a living from the stingy environment (for instance, water shortage, crop failure, insects, disease), these were secondary to the continuing losses sustained as a result of their many encounters with the exploiting Mormons.

Phase 2: Allotment (1920–1939)

In February of 1887 the U.S. Congress passed the Allotment Act. Under the provisions of this act, an individual Indian could receive a "trust patent" to certain acreages of land specifically designated for this purpose. Each qualifying individual could obtain a maximum of 160 acres of nonirrigable, grazing land. Trust patents were designed to expire after twenty-five years, at which time the allottee could receive full title to the land, unless the president chose to extend the trust period. To date, patents have been extended annually by Executive Order.

Prior to 1920 only one Navajo in Rimrock had applied for an allotment. However, between 1920 and 1940 most of the male heads of households had applied for and received 160-acre plots. Alloting agents were sent out to protect the Indians' rights in land transactions, but native American allotments were interspersed between those that were privately owned, or state lands, on in the public domain, a situation that resulted in a "checkerboarding" effect. This in turn created additional confusion for the Navajos.

In 1929 the Navajo Tribe purchased eighteen sections of

land just south of Rimrock for the specific use of local Navajos. A few years later Navajos were leasing state lands for grazing purposes, but as far as actual ownership and control, the tribal-purchase lands and the individual allotments obtained during this period, with some few exceptions, finalized Navajo land acquisition in the Rimrock area.

In 1924 the Bureau of Indian Affairs instituted a chapter system under which Navajo communities elected a local president, vice-president, and secretary, and regularly scheduled chapter meetings were to be held. The Rimrock Chapter was organized accordingly. Previous to this, local leadership had been primarily of an informal nature. Local informants claim that in the final decade of the last century one of the Anglo traders at Rimrock had convinced the Navajos of their need for a leader. Following this suggestion, supposedly, several of the Indians congregated and chose one of their elders, Many Beads, as the "Head Man." While the role was never clearly defined, the weight of the office and the influence of Many Beads's family tended to monopolize the position, persisting over the years and giving some direction to local activities. So strong was traditon along this line, that not until the mid-forties did the formally elected chapter officers wield sufficient influence to prevail over that of the informally recognized head man.

In 1927 the Rimrock Navajos were placed under the jurisdiction of the newly established Eastern Navajo Agency at Crownpoint, New Mexico. Prior to this, they had been largely ignored by both the tribe and the government's Bureau of Indian Affairs.

Even after the agency was established, officials visited Rimrock only infrequently and, because of the distance and traveling difficulties, Navajos from there rarely made the trip to Crownpoint. When they did, it was usually to seek assistance in resolving land-encroachment problems. The Navajos of Rimrock continued to feel neglected.

Nonetheless, in 1928, when the first official Navajo Tribal census was taken, the Rimrock residents were included. During

The old chapter house.

The new chapter house

the next two years they also were assigned official census numbers, and the groundwork was laid for a more meaningful participation in tribal life.

The early 1930s were difficult years for the Rimrock Navajos. The disastrous snowfall of 1931 brought death and starvation in its wake. Deflated prices caused by the national depression lowered local-produce income. New Anglo settlers from Texas arrived and in the process of establishing themselves, put new pressures on the Navajos and their land holdings.

In the midst of their problems, however, the Rimrock Navajos were greeted by new and expanded government assistance. Additional land was leased specifically for their use. Dams, wells, and roads were constructed. A "Rimrock Community Area" was organized under the Taylor Grazing Act of 1934, and under this act, no fees were to be charged on grazing permits for public-domain property in specific districts. The primary effect of all these activities was to give the federal government direct control over Indian and public land in the region. However, at the same time it did curtail the use of these lands by non-Indians.

Navajo stock reductions of the thirties were enforced by the government to correlate the number of animals with the actual carrying capacity of the land and thus limit the evident damaging effects of overgrazing on Navajo forage acreage. Range specialists were employed to calculate the carrying capacity of each district, and limits were set in numbers of "sheep units year long" (S.U.Y.L.). Grazing permits were then issued, based on the carrying capacity of the district and the amount of land held by an individual. One sheep unit was equivalent to one goat, one-fifth horse, and one-fourth cow, and, dependent on the number of S.U.Y.L.'s stipulated in his permit, a permittee could proportion his livestock in any way he so desired, so long as the total units did not exceed the limit permitted. Each fall, if his herd had increased beyond the allotted quota, the owner was required to reduce his stock by selling enough animals to regain permit levels.

Bitterness followed the enforced reductions and, although this feeling has in some cases persisted among the Navajos, there are those in the Rimrock group who admit that it had been necessary. One of the older stockmen in the area, Charles Yazi, recalls:

> I had 1,600 sheep, but they knocked it down to 320. That's all they allotted me; and three horses, a team and a saddle horse. Some people, they fight with them, that John Collier [Commissioner of Indian Affairs at that time]; they fight with them at Window Rock, but I think it was right. We had been overgrazing.

The stock-reduction program, along with other mandatory government designs, served a positive function in helping to convince the Rimrock Navajos that, in many respects, "Washington was on their side." This awareness led to a new confidence, and Navajos in the Rimrock community became more aggressive in their relations with whites.

The second phase of Rimrock-Navajo history saw the establishment of family groups on alloted lands, official recognition of the Rimrock Chapter by tribal authorities, greater government assistance and intervention, and the birth of a new sense of determination and community awareness. Because of increased interaction with forces outside the area, such as the tribe and the federal government, the Rimrock Navajos began to see themselves as a unique and distinctive group.

Phase 3: Definition (1940-1969)

Technically, this phase was initiated in the fall of 1939 with the election of a delegate from Rimrock to represent the Rimrock Navajo Community in the newly reorganized Navajo Tribal Council. Although this new involvement in tribal affairs eventually led to a new sense of political purpose among the Rimrock group, early participation on the Council was a disappointment to local representatives who felt their particular problems were being ignored.

In 1942, feelings of unhappiness and neglect generated by the tenuous relationship that persisted between the Crownpoint Agency and the Rimrock Navajos prompted the latter to petition for transfer of their jurisdiction to the United Pueblos Agency in Albuquerque and the subagency in Blackrock, near Zuni. The transfer was effected, and the close proximity of the subagency led to new benefits, improved services, and better relations with the Bureau of Indian Affairs.

In 1952 the Mormon village of Rimrock constructed new high-school facilities, and the following summer the Bureau of Indian Affairs began construction of dormitory buildings in the northeast section of town on land donated by one of the men in the community. Upon its completion in 1954, the dormitory opened with some one hundred Navajo children as boarders. Of the new employees, which included a director, several aides, maintenance personnel, and cooks, about half were Native Americans from the surrounding area.

The dormitory facilities

That same fall the Bureau of Indian Affairs contracted with the Rimrock schools for the education of the one hundred Navajo students. This was the first time that there had been any substantial number of Indian children in the Rimrock school system. Prior to this, only a few Navajo youngsters who lived in the immediate vicinity of the community had attended classes in town. For the most part, those who received any formal schooling at all had gone either to the Day School—facilities constructed by the B.I.A. in 1946 about thirteen miles southeast of Rimrock for the purpose of providing a basic elementary education for local Navajo children—or to B.I.A. or mission schools located in other more remote areas. Within ten years the terms of the original contract were expanded to include two hundred Navajo students in the Rimrock schools. Overcrowding occurred in both the dormitory and the schools, however, and a perpetual limit of one hundred and fifty was established.

In the early 1950s the additional opportunities afforded by opening the Rimrock dormitory and school to the Navajos began to produce a dramatic effect on Navajo literacy rates and educational levels. The latter, in turn, resulted in additional economic benefits. Better equipped for industrial jobs, young Indians began to migrate to "the city" and better employment opportunities.

From a demographic perspective, Kluckhohn and Morgan have defined the principal characteristics of this period in Rimrock-Navajo history as the fragmentation of original family groups or outfits.[14] This fragmentation resulted primarily from the death of heads of outfits and also from the dispersion of sibling groups.

Increasing population also placed a growing burden on community resources. While this "fragmentation" phenomenon tended to redefine the structure of individual family groups by diminishing the number of members in each unit and creating new leadership, it should not be interpreted as a disintegration of local social life. In many ways, this process was simply one expression of the broadening sense of interrelatedness, as the Rimrock Navajos began to place less emphasis on traditional kinship ties and devote more attention to their existence as a unique, functioning community.

During the 1950s and early 1960s, the Rimrock Navajos became more deeply involved in the life of the Rimrock village itself as well as in the large communities directly to the north. Also, influenced by the government, missionaries, travelers, anthropologists, and teachers, they began to broaden their interests beyond the confines of their immediate area.[15] This budding secularism or incipient cosmopolitanism was prompted by additional factors such as education, travel, new occupational opportunities, and the overall development of the Rimrock area.

In 1963, census records of the Rimrock Navajos were transferred from the United Pueblos Agency in Albuquerque to the Navajo Agency headquarters at Window Rock, Arizona. The move was a critical one, for with the establishment of a "Rimrock Chapter Community Census" came other benefits, such as participation in special Navajo programs and work projects.

In 1968 Rimrock High School, because of low enrollment and inadequate science and library facilities, was closed by the state of New Mexico. Navajo parents were forced to have their children bussed to Zuni High School, to send them to boarding school in other areas, or simply to keep them at home. During the following year, Rimrock was the scene of several incidents centering around the problem of education.

Navajo parents, represented by the D.N.A. (*Dinébehna Naxxlna bee Agabitaxé,* "People's Legal Service," an organization funded by the O.N.E.O. that provides legal aid for the Navajo people), filed suit against the state of New Mexico to force reopening of the Rimrock school. They also pressured the government to provide additional dormitories closer to the homes of the Navajo children than the present Rimrock facilities. Although these efforts failed to gain the expected results, in 1969 the District Court ruled that county schools must furnish transportation for all students living within county boundaries, including those Navajo children living in areas remote from the main highways.

In general, this phase in Rimrock-Navajo history was characterized by the definition of the group's role within the structure of Navajo tribal-political life at large. Along with increased tribal participation came greater attention from, and rapport with, government agencies, a new involvement in the village activities of Rimrock, and a stronger sense of unity as a distinct political entity. Again, additional education, mobility, and economic opportunities manifested clear trends toward modernization.

Phase 4: A New Sense of Community (1970–?)

Late in 1969, a young D.N.A. lawyer working in the Rimrock area for the Tribe took it upon himself to organize an all-Indian school board and to solicit funds from various private and government agencies for the creation of a genuinely Navajo high school, to be operated by and for The People. After some ambitious negotiations, a total of $328,000 was obtained, the old high-school building was leased from the town, and plans for the opening of the Rimrock Navajo High School were well underway.

A loosely organized summer-school program was engineered by the founding director in June 1970, and in September the new high school began formal operation with approximately one hundred and thirty students, only twenty per cent of whom were Anglo. A creative curriculum was instituted that included courses in Navajo language and culture.

From the beginning of the school's program, local Anglo parents voiced complaints about the organization's operation. They were unhappy about not being given a role in school affairs. The character and qualifications of the faculty also disturbed them, and many of the instructors, some of whom had been recruited from other professional backgrounds and other areas of the country, were labeled as "hippies" or "troublemaking Easterners." There was also a concern that the members

Rimrock Navajo High School.

The elementary school.

of the high-school administration were not adequately trained in professional education.

The fall of 1970 witnessed the continued polarization of the two groups : local whites (mainly the Mormons) versus Rimrock Navajo High School. At the dedication of remodeled facilities, an event occurred that received wide publicity. A handful of local Anglos and an Albuquerque journalist alleged that several of the new high-school teachers refused to stand during the pledge of allegiance. This, coupled with the contention that militance and revolution were being taught in the high school, instigated a flurry of newspaper articles, editorials, letters, and a host of charges and countercharges.

As the controversy raged, new charges were leveled by both the high-school directors and the townspeople. The former loudly denied each and every point in the Anglo attack and in turn accused local whites of putting personal interests ahead of those of the community as a whole. Their opponents, with an ad hoc school-board committee as spokesman, voiced additional charges concerning the inadequacies of the school program, the supposed discrimination against white students, and alleged "puppet" or "rubber-stamp" role of the Navajo school board itself. As antagonisms continued to broaden the communications gap, most of the white parents withdrew their children from the school and enrolled them at Zuni, leaving only a handful of white pupils in the school. With the removal of Anglo students, the whites consoled themselves by assuming an affected sympathetic attitude toward the problems of the school and its enrollment, and polemics began to cool.

At this time, however, the State Board of Education stepped into the picture, demanding that the new high school meet their accreditation standards or face a severe penalty. In the first place, until the high school was officially accredited, it would not be eligible for any state aid or textbook assistance, nor could its athletic teams compete with any other schools in the state. Again, as a final blow, if the school refused to cooperate, or was unable to meet minimum standards, the state threatened to take action against any parents continuing to send their children to the deficient institution. After weeks of investigation, discussion, and compromise, the state agreed, in January 1971, to issue temporary accreditation, with the understanding that the school would do all possible to correct any existing problems.

The year 1971 saw two other significant events in the lives of the Rimrocks Navajos. In February, one of the Navajo High School directors was elected to the county school board, and in April the Rimrock Chapter petitioned the Navajo Tribal Council for official inclusion as a part of the reservation, a request that, as of August 1973, had yet to be confirmed.

In the spring of 1972, FM station KTDB began broadcasting from studios located near the chapter offices south of Rimrock. Under the direct control of local Navajos, the station provides people in the area with a wide range of music, especially country-western and traditional, as well as many special-interest features and local news, all in Navajo. Financed by government and private funding, KTDB has served to reinforce the fundamental forces toward political unity among Rimrock Navajos.

For years, the two largest Rimrock populations—the Anglo Mormons and the Navajos—have lived in two completely different worlds. While there were routine contacts between members of both societies in work, in trading, or through mission activities, the broader community experience over the years manifested a radical separateness.

Still, the daily casual interactions reinforced feelings of superiority on the one hand, and of resentment and hostility on the other. Because of political and economic realities, the Rimrock Navajos, until recently, almost fatalistically resigned themselves to an inferior position.

Events in recent years, however, have begun to rearrange many of the habits ingrained by history. Common interest in the area's economic development, the new Navajo High School, and the increasing effectiveness of Indian political power have all served to create a core of concern that has in turn realigned local power and has forced the two groups to operate as a single

The developing Rimrock chapter headquarters.

B.I.A. Headquarters in Rimrock.

community. Despite the friction surrounding the issues, these events seem to portend a new era in local affairs as the Navajos continue to appreciate their potential as a viable political unit.

GENERAL CULTURAL ORIENTATION: 1970

Many significant changes have taken place in the life of Rimrock-Navajo society since the Many Beads and Cojo families settled in the area following the Fort Sumner captivity. The last two decades have been especially dramatic and critical. In addition to many economic and ideological developments (to be treated in the following two chapters), the following changes have been observed: population has increased, housing and living conditions have improved, social organization and residence patterns have been modified, and education has become an expected rather than a unique alternative.

The dam and the reservoir on the northwest corner of town.

Population

Population totals for the Rimrock Navajos have always been subject to difficulty. As a result, no one had ever really been sure how many Navajos there were in Rimrock, although, thanks to the work of Kluckhohn, Spuhler and Kluckhohn, and Morgan, more is known about the demographic history of this group than any other comparable Navajo population.[16] Still, for any given year, it is difficult to get an exact figure. For example, in 1950 the B.I.A. published two totals for the Rimrock Navajos: a tribal total of 597 and a service total of 575.[17] On the other hand, Kluckhohn contends that there were 625 of The People in the Rimrock area that year.[18] Because the latter figure is based on more accurate data-collecting methods and is more in keeping with comments by local informants, I am inclined to rely more heavily on Kluckhohn's total.

A similar problem exists with the available 1970 population totals for the Rimrock Navajos. The tribe, in conjunction with the B.I.A. published a figure of 1,389 persons for this area in April of that year. In October the Rimrock Office of the B.I.A. released its annual report in which a total of 1,234 was cited. According to officials, both of these are "service totals" and refer

Table 3

Rimrock=Navajo population (1970)*

(By age groups)	
Under 16	585
16–34	373
35–65	224
65 and over	52
Total	1,234
Labor force	507

* Figures taken from B.I.A., Reservation Population Support Capacity Study (1970).[19]

to actual residents of the area. I believe that the discrepancy here lies in the inadequacy of the tribal records. Also, because the smaller figure tends to agree more closely with my observations, I am accepting the latter as the more accurate of the two (*see* Table 3).

Assuming that these totals for the Rimrock Navajos —625 (1950) and 1,234 (1970)—bear some semblance of reality, one can calculate a 3,500 per cent increase in population for the period since 1880 and a ninety-seven per cent increase over the past twenty years. The latter figure agrees generally with the percentage growth statistic of the reservation as a whole for the same two decades—64,274 (1950) and 126,625 (1970).

Housing

By 1970 the Rimrock Navajos had witnessed many changes in housing styles and conditions relative to both 1880 and 1950. In the first place, there were seven Navajo families living in frame houses within the village limits of Rimrock itself in 1970, as opposed to none in 1950. Again, several had built conventional houses along the main highway, two to five miles east of Rimrock.

For those Navajos living in the more remote regions of the area, there were still hogans, *chaha'oh's*, and corrals, but with many critical modifications. In most households, hogan styles were much more varied. Besides the traditional dome-shaped type with its dirt roof and floors, the Navajos were building log hogans with plywood roofs and concrete floors. Others were fashioning one-room frame buildings in hogan style with shingled roofs and either wooden or concrete floors. All together there were approximately twelve different styles of hogans in the area, encompassing a wide range of feature variations, as modern building methods and materials were applied to traditional designs.

An old-style hogan.

The chaha'oh.

A "brush hogan."

A cooking shelter.

A remodeled hogan.

With the exception of the sweathouse, the other traditional structures were still found in the typical "cluster" in 1970. The roughly constructed corral housed the family livestock. The log cabin provided extra space either for sleeping or cooking. The *chaha'oh* continued to be used as a shade and a place to prepare food in the summer. It also served to house many daily activities when the hogan was being used for ritual or ceremonial activities.

There were very few sweathouses left in the area. The church had been perhaps the strongest influence acting toward their demise. According to local informants, only a few of the older, traditional Navajos in the more remote regions of the area still participated in sweatbath activities. As a result, the small dirt-and-log structure was seldom seen in the contemporary arrangement of Navajo living quarters in Rimrock.

Another recent development in the Rimrock-Navajo housing situation is the entry of both the tribe and the federal government into the attempt to improve Indian living standards. Under the auspices of the Office of Navajo Economic Opportunity (O.N.E.O.), the Housing Improvement Training Program (H.I.T.P.) has, since 1968, been selectively building new two- and three-bedroom frame houses and making improvements on other homes in the Rimrock area. The H.I.T.P. was structured originally to provide on-the-job vocational training and income for unemployed members of the local work force, and on each project the program furnishes the labor and a limited amount of the materials necessary. In addition to this, the B.I.A. has begun to furnish conventional housing, so that many Navajo families in the Rimrock area have recently obtained, at no cost to themselves, new or improved-standard housing—"standard" here being defined in terms of B.I.A. and O.N.E.O. regulations.

The new housing has not been met with complete approval by the Rimrock Navajos. Many families, especially the older ones, continue to live in hogans adjacent to the new houses, while others use the more modern structures only seasonally. Several of the elderly Navajos have expressed dissatisfaction with the O.N.E.O. and B.I.A. homes because of their failure to conform to traditional patterns. Nanabah Coho, an older lady in the community, after spending several nights in her newly constructed concrete-block unit, moved back into her old hogan, complaining that the new building completely confused her daily schedule : "In the hogan the sun comes through the smoke-hole in the morning, and I know when to start my day."

Another program, under the sole sponsorship of the tribe, that has had a noticeable impact on Rimrock housing conditions and patterns is the Ten-Day Project.[20] One of the several functions of this program is that of building new hogans where needs are evident. These dwellings are generally of logs, hexagonal in shape, neatly and sturdily constructed, roofed with sheet plywood, and shingled.

Despite the dimensions of these recent efforts, the overall housing conditions in 1970 were far from adequate. According to B.I.A. figures, less than two percent of eligible families in the area were currently living in housing meeting government standards, although over ten per cent were living in renovated units.[21]

Utilities

Adequate utilities were still a rarity for the Rimrock Navajos in 1970. Only about fifteen percent had electricity, and none of the Indians, in the rural areas had sewerage facilities or running water. Just one Navajo family had a telephone. The Rural Electric Association (R.E.A.) in New Mexico began wiring and servicing the homes of Navajos that met certain standards in 1968. In many cases, well-constructed hogans were qualifying for the service, and in spite of the costs involved, many of the Navajo families were making application. Water was still hauled by pickup truck or wagon from one of the fifteen wells in the area.

Material Culture

Traditionally, the Rimrock Navajos made a number of objects from stone, metal, hides, wool, plants, wood, horn, bone, and clay. There were bows and arrows, digging sticks, knives, scrapers, drills, smoothers, containers, pots, clothing, bedding, shields, waterbags, jewelry, and baskets.

By 1950 the material culture of the Navajos had changed dramatically in relation to traditional patterns in the Rimrock area. Kluckhohn recorded many of the changes.[22] Pottery had not been made since 1938. No bow and arrow had been made or used in the area since 1936. Only four or five elderly men still made and wore moccasins, and home manufacture was increasingly giving way to trading-post buying. Native foods, with the exception of some sheep and corn dishes, were no longer being prepared in the old way. Items employed for ceremonial and ritual purposes were still being made, "but the number of individuals who have requisite knowledge decreases each year."[23]

In the period around 1950, the Rimrock Navajos were very rapidly developing modern tastes in the areas of manufactured hardgoods and machinery. Most of them were buying factory-made clothing, some items of furniture, and assorted toys and household paraphernalia. By 1950 more than thirty homes had iron bedsteads. By 1952, thirty-nine automobiles, the majority of which were pickup trucks, were owned by local Navajos.[24] That same year they had three Massey-Ferguson tractors and planters and thirty-five plows and cultivators.

In 1970 the material culture of the Rimrock Navajos, while still traditional in elements such as building styles, decor, tools —such as carding and weaving devices—and in the lack of many modern appliances and conveniences, was even more persistent in its modernizing trends. Most food items were bought at the trading post or in nearby city supermarkets, although traditional menus such as mutton stew and fry bread prevailed. Clothing and some pieces of furniture were purchased in department stores as far away as Albuquerque. By 1970 there were more than 150 operational, Navajo-owned automobiles in the area, again almost ninety percent of them pickups. There were two or three more tractors than there were in 1950, but, due to the steady demise of farming in the area over the previous two decades, the number of plows and cultivators had not increased significantly.

Roberts lists 578 items found in his material inventory of the *Three Navajo Households* in the Rimrock area.[25] In the average household in 1970, one would have found most of the same items, with other more recent additions. Generally, there were more clothes—especially children's pants, shirts, and dresses

—cluttering the several dwellings of the typical cluster, stacked or unceremoniously draped along one side of a bare wall. Many of these items had been obtained through the "good will" of local missionary programs, and in some cases had never been worn in their second-hand status. In 1970 one would also have found more books, Bibles, pamphlets, and old magazines. By then, most families owned at least one battery-operated radio and an alarm clock. Again, there were fewer traditional medicines, but each family had its "bag of keepsakes," usually containing a few small pouches of pollen, pieces of flint, and some feathers. This item, for most local Navajos, had more sentimental meaning than medicinal or spiritual value. Outside the average hogan, one would also have seen more automobile parts, junked cars, trucks, discarded cans, papers, boxes, machinery, and old furniture.

Social Organization

Patterns of Kinship

Rimrock-Navajo social organization is essentially that of Navajo society as a whole, and the changes occurring in traditional patterns in Rimrock are for the most part those taking place throughout Navajo land.[26]

Descent among the Navajos is matrilineal. Kinship terminology manifests the following characteristics: (1) separate terms for cross- and parallel-cousins, the latter designated as brother or sister; (2) mother's sister and father's brother designated as mother and father, respectively, while separate terms are employed to refer to mother's brother or father's sister; and (3) separate terms for maternal grandparents (male and female), but only one designation for paternal grandparents. The mother's brother is traditionally the disciplinarian and male-parental authority, joking relationships prevail between several kinship categories (for example, male and female cross-cousins), and mother-in-law and son-in-law contact is strictly avoided.

For dealing specifically with the Rimrock situation, Kluckhohn has defined three functional social entities: the unit, the group, and the outfit.[27] By "unit" he had reference to the persons ordinarily living together, though not all in the same dwelling, "who share meals, chores, and—to some extent—possessions." The group "consists of two or more units that live within a radius of a few miles and are in frequent interaction." The primary criteria by which the outfit is defined are the special occasion and the leader. It is the group of relatives, wider than the extended family, that regularly pools its resources for major events such as ceremonials and sheep shearing. The outfit is generally identified in terms of its leadership.[28]

A traditional unit south of Rimrock.

In 1950 there were 125 units, fourteen groups, and seven outfits in the Rimrock area. Since that time, the population increase, the fragmentation of local outfits, and the modification of residence patterns has led to a substantial increase in the number of units.[29] In 1970 the Rimrock Navajos were distributed in a total of over 150 roughly defined units.

Clanship is still an important consideration among the Rimrock Navajos. A child is born into his mother's clan and automatically afforded a sense of solidarity and group identity extending well beyond the immediate family. Fellow clan members are addressed by the same kinship terms used to identify biological relatives of the same sex and age.

In 1948, nineteen of a total of more than fifty Navajo clans were represented in Rimrock, the four largest comprising seventy-seven percent of the total population.[30] By 1953 this figure had risen to twenty-one.[31] Recent years have seen the entry of members of previously unrepresented clans into the Rimrock area. Marriages with outsiders and several local job opportunities have been responsible for the increase, and in 1970 there were at least twenty-four Navajo clans represented among the Rimrockites, the most populous still being the Meadow, Bitter Water, and Alkaline Water groups.

Although clan identification serves to put personal relations into perspective as Rimrock residents increasingly come in contact with Navajos from other areas, its primary function is still that of regulating marriage. While Rimrock Navajos are very much aware of clan membership and its importance for marriage protocol, the significance and rationale underlying clan linkage has for most of them been lost. While traditionally certain clans have been loosely related by virtue of common historical event, the majority of The People in Rimrock do not know what clans are linked to either their own or their father's.

The customary matrilineal orientation of Navajo social organization, reflected in lineage, ownership, and inheritance patterns, is slowly undergoing modification among the Rimrock Navajos. Gary Witherspoon argues that, in general, "Navajo social organization is ordered by the cultural definitions of motherhood."[32] On the other hand, the use of the English language and paternally inherited surnames, the adoption of Western marriage and residence patterns, the new role of wage-working males, the allotment of land in the names of fathers, boarding-school education, and expanding settlement alternatives have had a dramatic effect on conceptual patterns of social organization in the Rimrock area. To say the least, the matrilineality of Navajo society is being threatened to the point that such a blanket classification is of questionable meaning. While still functioning to define relationships and individual rights among the older traditionalists in the community, increasingly the tendency is becoming simply a relic of the kinship terminology. In reality, actual behavior seems to defy categorization.

Residence

David Aberle records a statistical preference for matrilocal residence among the Navajos as of the 1930s.[33] According to his figures, two-thirds of the families were matrilocal, one-ninth patrilocal, and two-thirds mixed in their choice of postmarital residence.[34]

For 1950, in the Rimrock area, Kluckhohn observed a less clear-cut preference.[35] Out of ninety-seven cases, forty-seven were uxorilocal, thirty-three virilocal, six bilocal, and eight neolocal. Fifteen years later the situation had varied to a degree. According to the data furnished by Reynolds, Lamphere, and Cook on eighty-nine married couples in the Rimrock area, residence was as follows: uxorilocal, thirty-nine; virilocal, twenty-four; neolocal, eighteen; and other, eight.[36] This tendency toward neolocality was even more evident in 1970. Increasingly, young Navajo married couples, if they chose to remain in the Rimrock area, were establishing homes independent of either set of parents.

Marriage

In the traditional past, Navajo marriages were arranged by the parents of the two parties involved. The event itself was marked by a simple ceremony and, in most cases, an exchange of property between the two families ensued. In many cases there was a reciprocating arrangement in which a family giving a son in marriage to the daughter of another family could expect to see the marriage of a younger daughter to a younger son from the other family at a later date.

Polygyny was a normal alternative, divorce was frequent, and second marriages were generally "affairs" that simply led eventually to a stable relationship.

By 1950 the nuptial pattern in Rimrock was at variance with the older norms. Only sixty percent of marriages were arranged by parents. Since 1940 there had been seven non-arranged marriages between local and Reservation students in relationships that had developed in the boarding-school environment. Again, only nine men in Rimrock were still living with two wives in 1950.[37]

Marriage was statistically less traditional in 1970 than it had been twenty years before in Rimrock. By this time, only two men were openly living with two wives—in both these cases, sisters. Pressure from both the Anglo and Navajo communities had tended to eliminate the polygynous union as a marital alternative. In two cases in which men gave up one of their wives, one of the two women involved simply demanded that the husband make a choice and limit his activities to one spouse. The influence of the Nazarene mission had reinforced the new monogamous tendencies.

Some marriages in the Rimrock area were still arranged and solemnized in the traditional fashion, but most couples made their own decisions, and many had been turning to civil or church ceremonies. With an increasing number of young Navajos going away to school, the unarranged liaison with outsiders was becoming more frequent, and, due to the general feeling that geographical mobility had certain economic advantages, it was viewed favorably by most parents.

According to the customary rules of marriage, a Navajo should not marry, in order of restriction: (1) a member of his own clan; (2) a member of his linked-clan group; (3) a member of his father's clan; (4) a member of his father's linked-clan group; or (5) an individual whose father is a member of his own father's clan.[38]

By 1970 the Rimrock Navajos seemed little concerned about customary propriety in the business of taking a mate. Awareness of clan-group significance had faded, the importance of father's clan membership was frequently overlooked, and the only rule retaining any serious social proscription was the first one : a Navajo should not marry a member of his own clan. While the explanation given for incest rules prohibiting members of the same family from marrying was usually biological, the defense of the prohibition of intraclan marital ties was social. If a person married a member of his own clan, his children would not have a clan. This was still tantamount to nonbeing in Navajo society.

In assessing the social-organization picture in Rimrock for the 1950 period, Kluckhohn made the following observation :

> In general, the greater the influence of European culture the greater the probability that residence will be virilocal or neolocal and the greater the tendency toward "weak" social organization.[39]

While there is still a latent feeling, though seldom expressed, that old patterns ought to be preferred, the growing modernization of the Rimrock-Navajo community has given its young people a new freedom, mobility, and sense of independence that are continuing to "weaken" the traditional socal organization.

Political Organization

Some of the most evident changes in the process of Navajo acculturation have been witnessed in the area of The People's political life. Many Anglo-American methods in the organization and administration of power have been completely foreign to the traditional Navajo mind. For this reason, even by 1950, the political organization of the Rimrock Navajos was still predicated on the mechanics of customary patterns of community interaction.

Power has tended to be in the hands of older people who are still in full possession of their faculties, of the more wealthy, or singers. The exercise of power is seldom overt and direct but rather masked, oblique, and diffuse. Evident power, like evident wealth, is a cause of jealousy and an invitation either to attack by witches or to gossip that the holder is a witch.[40]

During the years of the late 1940s, the importance of chapter organization in Rimrock was assuming a new significance, and meetings were being held as many as twenty times a year. Chapter elections led to the polarization of "conservative" and "progressive" factions in the community, and heated debate and controversy boiled around the related issues.

By 1970, Rimrock-Navajo politics had taken on new and expanded characteristics. Power was being exercised by the wealthy members of the community. The influence of singers and the traditionally wise had been gradually diminishing and it was becoming easier to overlook and ignore these few voices from out of the past. Because of the strong influence of the church and increased educational opportunities and achievement in the area, the fear of witchcraft no longer served to restrain, at least to the extent it had earlier, exhibitions of individual power.

According to unconfirmed reports and rumors in 1964, when Rimrock's current tribal-council representative first ran for that office, he bribed members of the Community Action Committee (C.A.C.), the group responsible for ballot counting in local elections. Regardless of the veracity of these contentions, it is true that he has increasingly assumed an almost dictatorial role in local-chapter proceedings, guiding policy through the use of both his wealth and his personally selected henchmen. Because of the power of the machine he has created, many of the Rimrockites previously playing an active role in local politics have been intimidated into silence. With the return of Rimrock's educated young Navajos, however, others are beginning to speak out, and the display of naked force typical of the 1970 period may soon be modified, and local politics may revert to more reasoned and collective styles of action.

The Rimrock Navajos no longer had a local judge in 1970, but the police force had been expanded into a larger and more efficient unit with four officers. Defining jurisdiction was a major problem, especially where a felony was involved. Because of the confusing nature of checkerboard-land status, several cases had been stalled for months in court proceedings over the issue of proper jurisdiction, which depends on an accurate statement as to exactly where the alleged crimes were committed.

The Navajo police in the Rimrock network operate under the auspices of the tribe and can handle all traffic matters and those problems and complaints involving Navajos in the area. Felony cases are referred to state and federal authorities, and most police work in the area is routine: stopping speeders, arresting drunks, breaking up fights, investigating petty larceny complaints, and patrolling public gatherings.

The year 1970 saw a dramatic increase of police activity, and complaints about the dereliction and incompetence of the officers themselves were frequent. Problems connected with the new high school—drinking, fighting, ganglike activities— brought added responsibilities and risks to the Rimrock force. During that summer one officer was severely beaten by a group of teen-age boys when he attempted to stop a fight. The police- men, on other occasions, were threatened and attacked verbally by bellicose members of the Navajo community, in particular the young. As a result of such intimidating incidents, the rumor that the "Rimrock cops were chicken" began to gain momentum. Whites and Indians alike complained that the policemen would often ignore calls or keep the phone "off the hook" to avoid their duty if they thought there might be any risk involved. During the large "squaw dance" that was held in the area in the early fall of 1970, no officer appeared during any of the three nights to help maintain order, a normal routine for tribal policemen on the Reservation. The immediate reaction again was that local law enforcers were afraid to risk confrontation.

General Acculturation

In 1950 the Rimrock Navajos were still very traditional in most of their behavior, in fact, probably more so than their relatives on the Reservation, due to less direct contact with outsiders, in particular educators, missionaries, and government personnel.

The first Rimrock Navajo to receive any formal education went to school in 1886. During a two-year matriculation at Fort Defiance, he managed to develop a 100-word English vocabulary. By 1905 the Rimrock group had ten of its young people attending Alburquerque Indian School. In 1950 only thirty-six men and twenty-eight women from Rimrock had attended school at all, and only two were high-school graduates. That same year, twenty-eight men and nine women could speak basic English, but only three of them had developed an interpretive facility.

Relative to other Navajos and Southwestern Indian groups, the Rimrock population has, until recently, received very little formal education. In 1946 only twelve percent of the Rimrock children between the ages of six and eleven were in school, as compared to 100 percent of the Shiprock Navajo and sixty-one percent of this age group at Navajo Mountain (*see* Table 4).

Table 4

Percent of children in the age group 6–11 in school (1946)[*]

Navajo	
Shiprock	100
Navajo Mountain	61
Rimrock	12
Papago	100
Zuni	100
Sioux	100
Hopi	100

By 1970 things had improved tremendously. Besides government and mission boarding schools, the opening of local public schools to the Navajos and the recent creation of the Rimrock

[*] Figures taken from Leighton and Kluckhohn.[41]

Navajo High School had had an impact on educational levels, literacy, and language ability in the area. According to B.I.A. figures, eighty-seven percent of all Rimrock-Navajo children between the ages of five and eight were in school during that year (*see* Table 5).

Table 5

Rimrock–Navajo children in school (1970)*

Age group	Number in school	Total	Percentages
Age 5	13	39	33
6–14	280	295	95
15–18	101	124	81
Total	394	458	86

On the basis of my sample, which represented almost forty-five percent of the total Rimrock-Navajo population, there were in 1970 almost 100 high-school graduates in the area.

With increased amounts of formal education has come a greater facility in language skills. According to the figures in the sample, better than fifty percent of the Rimrock group in 1970 had at least a basic English vocabulary. Again, most of the high-school graduates were very flexible in either language, Navajo or English, and exhibited varying degrees of interpretive ability.

In general, the twenty years from 1950 to 1970 saw the Navajo make large strides in their adjustment to today's progressive world. While still lagging behind certain other groups of their fellow tribesmen, increased education, travel, mobility, and contacts with the non-Indian world had radically altered the life-style of the Rimrock Navajos.

* Figures from B.I.A., Reservation Population Support Capacity Study.[42]

NOTES

1. Kluckhohn, "The Rimrock Navajo," p. 371.

2. Donald E. Worchester, "The Navajo during the Spanish Regime in New Mexico," *New Mexico Historical Review* 26, no. 2 (1951):103.

3. George D. Hammond and Agapito Rey, *Expedition into New Mexico Made by Antonio de Espejo, 1582–1583, as Revealed in the Journal of Diego Perez de Luxan, a Member of the Party* (Los Angeles: Quivaro Society, 1929), p. 72.

4. M. A. Stokes and T. L. Smiley, "Tree-ring Dates from the Navajo Land Claim, III. The Southern Sector," *Tree-Ring Bulletin* 27:3–4, 9–10.

5. Clyde Kluckhohn, "Aspects of the Demographic History of a Small Population," in *Estudios Anthropologicos,* ed. Juan Comas (Mexico City: Dirreccion General de Publicaciones, 1956), p. 359.

6. John P. Harrington, "Southern Peripheral Athapaskan Origins, Divisions, and Migrations," *Smithsonian Institute Miscellaneous Collections* 100 (1940):515.

7. Rimrock Files, 12 September 1943 (Santa Fe, New Mexico; Laboratory of Anthropology).

8. Indian Claims Commission, "Navajo Plaintiff Exhibit 3047 through 3068A, Docket 229," mimeographed (Window Rock, Arizona: Navajo Tribe, 29 June, 1970).

9. Indian Claims Commission, "Navajo Land Claim, Docket 229," mimeographed (Window Rock, Arizona: Navajo Tribe, 29 June 1970).

10. Kluckhohn, "Aspects of the Demographic History," pp. 363–64.

11. Kluckhohn, "The Rimrock Navajo," p. 346.

12. Kenneth Morgan, "A Genetic Demography of a Small Navajo Community" (Ph.D. diss., University of Michigan, 1968), p. 37.

13. Rimrock Files, 8 September 1947.

14. Kluckhohn, "Aspects of Demographic History," p. 357; Morgan, p. 39. The "outfit" is defined by Morgan as "including a married couple, their married children, and their married grandchildren." *See* Morgan, p. 39.

15. *See* chapter 2.

16. Kluckhohn, "Aspect of the Demographic History; Morgan; J. N. Spuhler and Clyde Kluckhohn, "Inbreeding Coefficents of the Rimrock-Navajo Population," *Human Biology* 25 (1953):295–317.

17. "Tribal population" includes all members of the tribe or segment of the tribe without reference to residence. "Service population" refers only to those members of the tribe living on reservation or tribal lands and who are thus eligible for government services.

18. Kluckhohn, "The Rimrock Navajo," p. 333.

19. Bureau of Indian Affairs, 'Reservation Population Support Capacity

Study," mimeographed (Window Rock, Arizona: Navajo Agency, 1970).

20. *See* chapter 6.

21. Bureau of Indian Affairs, "Reservation Population Support Capacity Study."

22. Kluckhohn, "The Rimrock Navajo." p. 345.

23. Ibid., p. 354.

24. Marion St. John, "Zuni, Navajo, and Spanish-American Economies" (Unpublished manuscript, Harvard University, 1952), p. 8.

25. John M. Roberts, "Three Navajo Households," *Peabody Museum Papers* 40, no. 3 (1951): 15–24.

26. *See* David Aberle, "Navajo," in *Matrilineal Kinship,* eds. David M. Schneider and Kathleen Gough (Berkeley and Los Angeles: University of California Press, 1961), pp. 96–201, for general discussion of Navajo social organization.

27. Kluckhohn, "The Rimrock Navajo," pp. 366–68.

28. Ibid.

29. T. R. Reynolds, L. Lamphere, and C. E. Cook, Jr., "Time, Resources, and Authority in a Navajo Community," *American Anthropologist* 69 (1967):189.

30. Kluckhohn, "The Rimrock Navajo," p. 358.

31. Guy J. Pauker, "Political Structure," in *People of Rimrock,* eds. E. Z. Vogt and E. M. Albert (Cambridge, Massachusetts: Harvard University Press, 1967), p. 205.

32. Gary Witherspoon, "A New Look at Navajo Social Organization," *American Anthropologist* 72 (1970):55–65.

33. Aberle, p. 155.

34. Ibid.

35. Kluckhohn, "The Rimrock Navajo," p. 364.

36. Reynolds, Lamphere, and Cook, p. 191.

37. Kluckhohn, "Tht Rimrock Navajo," p. 360.

38. Aberle, p. 146.

39. Kluckhohn, "The Rimrock Navajo." p. 369.

40. Ibid.

41. Dorothea C. Leighton and Clyde Kluckhohn, *Children of the People* (Cambridge, Massachusetts: Harvard University Press, 1948), p. 156.

42. Bureau of Indian Affairs, "Reservation Population Support Capacity Study."

2

Changing Woman versus Jehovah: The History of Religious Change in Rimrock

Changing Woman, the most notable figure in Navajo mythology, has seen her preeminence threatened in Rimrock in recent years by the invasion of enterprising Protestants and their supernatural triumvirate. As a result of these missionary efforts, Rimrock has become a hotbed of ideological turmoil and factionalism. This chapter is a description of this development.

TRADITIONAL RELIGION

The first difficulty that one encounters in attempting to treat Navajo religion is the fact that there is no word in Navajo equivalent to the English *religion*. This does not mean that The

People have ever wanted for religiosity. The spirit world, the myths, the ritual, and ceremonies of the Navajos combine to give them one of the richest and most comprehensive ideological systems among American Indians.

Because of the intricacy of the cultural content inherent in all areas of the system and the limitations of classic Western definitions of religion, many early students of the Navajos contended that The People had no area of thought or behavior that could legitimately be called *religious*. For example, Dr. Jonathon Letterman, a post surgeon at Fort Defiance in the 1850s, once observed of the Navajo that:

> Of their religion little or nothing is known as, indeed, all inquiries tend to show they have none; and even have not, we are informed, any word to express the idea of Supreme Being. We have not been able to learn that any perserverances of a religious character exist among them; and the general impression of those who have had means of knowing them is that, in this respect, they are steeped in the deepest degradation.[1]

However, with the advent of more comprehensive understandings of the religious phenomenon in the early twentieth century, the Navajo ideological system was treated more objectively, and scholars began to refer confidently to the reality of Navajo religion.

In a complex world of spiritual beings, myths, and ceremony, geared ultimately to the maintenance of personal health and harmony in the total world of the individual, lie the fundamental language and symbols of Navajo religious life. Changing Woman, Monster Slayer, the First People, Chantway myths, Blessing Way, Ghost Way, each reflect the total integration of Navajo culture, yet each is fraught with expressions of "ultimate concern" and symbolic attempts to structure an otherwise disorganized world.

The Rimrock Navajos have, historically, taken great pains to fulfill ritual and ceremonial obligations, carefully observing the complex obligations of traditional religious behavior.

Study in the Rimrock area indicates that adult men give one-fourth to one-third of their productive time to activities connected with the "priestly" rites; women, one-fifth to one-sixth. This is undoubtedly a higher proportion of time than most white people give to the church, the theatre, and the doctor combined, and it is excellent evidence of the importance of their religion to the Navajos.[2]

Religious Change

Despite the intensity of traditional religious activities in the Rimrock area, the period from 1940 to 1950 was one that saw many Navajos rejecting their native religion. During this decade the Nazarene missionaries began to work in the area, and the Mormons, who had been in Rimrock since the 1880s but who had had little success in converting the Navajos, renewed their efforts to baptize the Lamanites. Although increased participation in native ceremonies occurred in some circles as a result of "antagonistic acculturation to missionary activity" in Rimrock, the perod witnessed an overall decline in the importance of traditional Navajo religion.[3]

THE NAZARENE MISSION

The Church of the Nazarene, a small evangelical sect with a membership of approximately 400,000, first sent missionaries to the Rimrock Navajos in the fall of 1944. Since the mission was first organized, sixteen Anglo missionaries have worked in the area, Navajo membership has risen to almost 400, numerous buildings have been erected, and in general the Nazarenes have had a profound impact on all areas of Navajo life in Rimrock.

Program and Rationale

The Church of the Nazarene, a product of a nineteenth-century defection from the Methodist denomination, states its

main purpose as the recapturing of the true spirit of John
Wesley, the founder of Methodism. According to Nazarene
doctrine, a man must first be "saved" by the "forgiveness of his
sins," and then "sanctified holy" by the total consecration of his
life to God. This second experience is sometimes referred to as
"perfect love," and is the raison d'être of the movement. In
line with their emphasis on perfection, the Nazarenes are very
specific in defining proper ethical behavior. The following item
appeared in the monthly publication of the denomination's
North American Indian District:

> Avoid evil of every kind: including
> 1. Taking the name of God in vain
> 2. Profaning the Lord's day
> 3. Using of intoxication liquors as a beverage
> 4. Quarelling [sic], returning evil for evil, gossiping,
>   slandering, spreading surmises injurious to the good
>   name of others
> 5. The indulgence of pride in dress or behavior
> 6. Songs, literature, and entertainments not to the glory
>   of God; the theatre, the ballroom, the circus, and like
>   places.[4]

Among the Rimrock Navajos, the rodeo and traditional
ceremonies, such as the *Yeibichai* or the squaw dance, have been
added to the "evils" listed under number six in the above list.

The Nazarenes have had a full weekly program of activities
in the Rimrock mission for many years; Sunday school,
Sunday worship service, prayer meeting, young people's service,
missionary-society meetings, and training programs. The Sunday
services are the most important items on the weekly schedule
and last sometimes as long as seven hours. Sunday school begins
at 11:00 A.M. At noon they break for coffee, crackers, and
conversation, and the main service commences at 1:00 P.M. A
few gospel songs are sung from a small Navajo hymnal, the
offering is collected, and occasionally this is followed by a solo
rendition. After an extended public prayer, the pastor delivers

a short sermon, and the remainder of the service is scheduled for testimonies. Highly informal and with numerous interruptions, this portion of the program often lasts for several hours, many members testifying for as long as an hour. During the winter months it is usually dark outside before the service is dismissed.

Attendance at regular church services varies with the occasion. Special Sundays with their "covered-dish dinners" or gift giving usually find the mission stations filled to capacity. On the average Sunday, though, seventy-five percent or more of available seating space—the three stations have a combined seating capacity of between five and six hundred—is vacant. In general, the women outnumber the men more than two to one, and more than seventy-five percent of the average Sunday crowd will be women and children. This is similar to the situations Rapoport observed in the late 1940s in the Nazarene services in the Rimrock mission.[5]

Most of the Nazarene missionaries who have worked with the Rimrock Navajos have been motivated by what they refer to as "a call to the mission field." Convinced of the fact that the Navajos, like all other non-Western groups, are "lost in sin" and destined for hell unless they hear "the gospel story," the missionaries are firmly dedicated to the task of bringing the natives to "a knowledge of the saving grace of Jesus Christ." The rationale is well illustrated in a piece from the district monthly. A small Indian girl is dying and asks her father where she is going. As she cries, "Help me!",

> Father can tell her nothing. But the Indian man knew no more. Not even his love for his little girl enabled him to give her any hope. His heart was dark and filled with terror. And in this lonely hogan, the slender fingers tightened upon the father's hand, till they grew cold in death.
>
> They had not heard that the Son of God had come to this dark world that first Christmas morning to bring joy and peace to those who were in darkness and that through His death all people of all races could find Eternal Life.[6]

History

The early history of the Nazarene mission in Rimrock had been very thoroughly treated by Rapoport,[7] so for purposes of this investigation I am relying heavily on his material in analyzing the first phase of the evangelical group's activity in the area. Rapoport treated the Nazarene mission's establishment in the community in the period from 1945 to 1950 in four phases.[8] I am telescoping his time groupings into one *stabilization* phase (1945–1950) and describing two additional phases of my own : growth and prosperity (1951–1966), and decline, conflict, and stagnation (1967– ?).

Phase 1: Stabilization (1945–1950)
Rapoport called his first phase, "The Ingression" (January 1945–fall of 1946).[9] During this time the first missionary, the Rev. Fry, and his wife spent much of their time making initial contacts and getting established in the community. Using an interpreter, they visited the Navajos—usually the women, the infirm, and the aged—and attempted to tell the "Gospel story." Responses ranged from mild curiosity to open opposition by some of the more traditional.

In this same period, work was begun on a new building near the day school, some thirteen miles southeast of the Rimrock village. With the completion of the structure, which had a seating capacity of approximately 100, Rapoport began his second phase : "Spreading the Light" (fall of 1946–spring of 1948).[10] This was the "indoctrination" period as the missionaries began to systematically define the "issues." By 1947 there were Sundays when as many as eighty to ninety were in attendance. With a growing confidence that major success was imminent, the missionary put a heavy emphasis on the necessity of radical change. Rapoport notes that the missionaries believed that : Navajo religion was a pack of superstitions, its ceremonial practitioners engaged in "the devil's business.[11]

During the year 1947, a six-room house for the missionaries

and a three-room home for the interpreter were completed. Also, Fry began to hold services, several times a week, for the children at the day school—limited facilities provided by the tribe in 1946 to give Navajo children unable to go elsewhere a basic grade-school education. A Navajo board of trustees was selected for the new mission. Meanwhile, the new missionary began to get more heavily involved in community affairs. He spent time helping out at the new Navajo Cooperative Store, and took an active role in the election of chapter officers, placing his influence directly into the campaign of one of his church members running for office. This move put the religious issue squarely into the campaign and resulted eventually in a definite set back for his cause.

Rapoport's next phase, "The Time of Troubles" (early 1948 to 1949), had obvious roots in the previous period.[12] The election issues, Fry's hostility toward traditional Navajo values, and conflicts resulting from his adamant stand on the question of polygyny portended the reactions that this new phase was to bring. Campaign dialogue crystallized into clear-cut "conservative" versus "progressive" issues, and Fry's candidate was defeated, a definite blow to the Nazarene program. Under pressure from militant traditionalists, many Navajo "converts" disassociated themselves from the mission. During this same period Fry was caught in a scandal growing out of rumors that he had been involved in an extramarital romance with an Indian woman. This, coupled with the general disenchantment of the Navajo congregation concerning their missionaries, led to his resignation and departure in the spring of 1949.

Rapoport's final phase, "Period of Stabilization" (1949 through 1950), was initiated with the arrival of the new missionary, the Rev. Banks.[13] A soft-spoken individual, the new director of the mission, by his very timidity, made a favorable impression on the Navajo community. Unlike the loud and brash Fry, Banks treaded lightly where controversial issues were involved, and partly because of this, anti-mission hostilities began to subside, and church attendance began to increase.

This phase also saw the birth of a new sense of group identity among the Nazarene Navajos. They began to see themselves as a unique element within the community, and openly flaunted their "progressiveness."

> The strongest Galileans boasted that they no longer believed in ghosts, so were free to travel around at night without fear. They also made conscious and public attempts to debunk Navajo taboos such as mother-in-law avoidance.[14]

During the year 1950, several events took place that helped to stabilize Nazarene activities in the Rimrock area. Three of the Navajo converts were given local preacher's licenses. The Wycliff Translators came into the area and helped set up a reading program so that the Navajos could learn to read the Bible in their own language. Organization was improved, church activities were expanded, and the first campmeeting was held in Rimrock that summer.

By the end of 1950, the "settling-in" trauma had subsided, and with its new leadership and fresh enthusiasm, the Nazarene mission was firmly established in the Rimrock-Navajo community. As Rapoport prophetically observed, "barring catastrophic change, the program had stabilized for what appeared to be a long-term operating equilibrium."[15]

Phase 2: Growth and prosperity (1951–1966)

By 1951 the Rimrock-Nazarene Mission had eight-eight members, and Sunday-school attendance, a reliable index for measuring actual participation, was averaging seventy-seven. Total giving by the Navajo congregation had doubled since 1950 and reached almost one thousand dollars for the year. A missionary society was organized, and the local group was urged to support proselyting efforts in other parts of the world.

In the spring of 1952 the first Navajo-Nazarene funeral services were held, and, with the encouragement of the missionary, about forty of The People overcame traditional fears and attended.[16] Later that year the Banks left Rimrock, and a new missionary couple, the Harpers, took over the mission.

The next few years were rather uneventful ones for the Rimrock Nazarenes. Several families moved out of the area in 1953, and this, coupled with what appears to be an ineffectiveness on the part of the Harpers in working with the Navajos, stimulated a decline in attendance and income that year.

In 1954 the Footes replaced the Harpers at Rimrock and over the next five years, partly as a result of their popularity with the Navajos, brought new life to the Nazarene mission. Buildings were improved, Sunday-school and dormitory additions erected, and in October of 1958, an outpost, the Redlake Mission, was organized about seventeen miles south of the first establishment. A former ceremonial practitioner, who had had his local preacher's license for several years, was placed in charge. The new congregation, meeting in a recently constructed, corrugated-tin sanctuary, experienced several successes and threatened to overtake the older group in total attendance. Also during the Footes's tenure, a full-time nurse came to Rimrock to assist the missionaries, the first local Navajo was sent to a Nazarene college, and the Rimrock churches became the pride of the denomination's North American Indian District as attendance doubled and total giving tripled.

In the summer of 1959 the Footes left Rimrock and moved to Alabama where they took over the operation of a large chicken farm. They were replaced by the Blackmans, a couple who had previously worked with other Indian groups in the Southwest. Unlike Foote, who had related to the Navajos in a very personal way, the new missionary saw himself more as an "operator" and developed fewer close ties with the individual members of the mission. The impersonality and forcefulness of his role notwithstanding, the seven years of his stay in Rimrock saw several significant developments.

In September 1959 the original Rimrock mission was completely destroyed by fire. While it has never been verified, most of the Nazarenes in the area claim that it was the work of an arsonist, angered by their successes in the area. A new building was erected by the following April, reportedly "much larger and better than the one that burned."[17]

In 1960 Blackman got more involved in community affairs and controversy than any Nazarene missionary since Fry. One of the more dogmatic and outspoken of the Rimrock workers, he developed a reputation for personal attacks and public accusations of those members of the congregation who failed to conform completely to church standards and the local program. One of those stung by his fanaticism recalls:

> He was trying to take over. There was something about him I didn't like. . . . There were too many things he did and said that I didn't agree with. He kind of joked and teased a lot, but I never cared for that because I knew what he was like. He told people they were the devil and they were going to hell and things like that.

In the spring of 1960 Blackman was at odds with several of the personnel working at the B.I.A. dormitory in Rimrock. At this same time he began to attack the employees at the establishment from the mission pulpit and to stir up opposition among Navajo parents. He is reported to have accused personnel at the government facilities of putting the children to bed without clothes, beating them with iron cords, putting soap in their mouths, and hitting them with their fists. Under his direction, a telegram was sent to Washington listing twenty-seven specific accusations. As a result of the pressure from the missionary and his group of Navajo parents, the F.B.I. conducted a thorough investigation of the Rimrock dormitory, and the two factions in the controversy met in open hearings. In these public forums the Nazarene delegation demanded that all of the employees at the boarding facilities be immediately released.

While the "issues" were never really resolved, the opponents of the dormitory operation were informed that no action could be taken unless a petition, signed by at least three-fourths of the Navajo community, were to be filed with government authorities.

The logistical difficulties of such an undertaking cooled the ambitions of the Nazarene faction, and the debate soon faded, with few, if any, direct results.

In February 1962 the Rimrock mission burned to the ground for the second time. After this event, mission authorities decided to relocate, and nine acres of land were purchased on the eastern outskirts of the Rimrock village. During the remainder of the year, while the new building was being constructed, the Navajo congregation held their regular weekly services in the homes of different members. By the spring of 1963 a new Sunday-school building and a missionary parsonage were completed, and the new facilities were dedicated as the *Rimrock Onion Mission*.

The Nazarene mission in Rimrock.

In October 1963 the third outpost in the Rimrock area was erected and organized as the *Sand Mountain Mission*, twenty miles southeast of Rimrock. By this time all three stations had native pastors who were handling most of the preaching and weekly program responsibilities, the role of the missionary being limited to general organizational and leadership activities.

By 1964 the sanctuary at the Rimrock Onion Mission had been completed, and an additional missionary aide, Mrs. Hawk, had arrived to assist the Blackmans. With increasing attendance and a diversifying program, the Nazarene mission was beginning to exercise a broader influence in the Rimrock-Navajo community. Increasingly, Nazarene Navajos were being elected to tribal and chapter offices and assuming a larger share of community responsibility.

This phase of Nazarene-mission activity among the Rimrock Navajos came to a close at the end of the year 1966. In terms of internal harmony, community influence, and numerical and financial succes, this year was perhaps the high point of the Nazarene work in Rimrock. It was befitting that Rimrock Onion was named the "Church of the Year" on the denomination's North American Indian District.

Phase 3: Decline, conflict, and stagnation (1957–?)
Decline (1967–1969)

Early in 1967 the Blackmans left Rimrock, and Mrs. Hawk was placed in charge of local Nazarene-mission activities. Despite the fact that membership and attendance increased during the next two years, the program began to develop a number of problems. As some of the less-committed Navajos began to shirk responsibilities connected with appointed jobs and elected offices in the mission, the more established members began to complain, and factions developed in the individual stations. These grew into larger issues and disputes, and additional difficulties arose in early 1968 when the Rimrock-Onion membership voted to remove their Navajo pastor from his position, blaming him for the prevailing discontent and factionalism. He was replaced by an employee from the Nazarene Training School in Albuquerque, a Potawatomi

Indian who had married a Rimrock-Navajo girl. Not content to limit the deposed preacher's punishment to his removal, many members of the congregation continued to make his life miserable, accusing him of immorality and mistreating his family. In 1969 the rejected pastor hanged himself, and his few remaining friends and family bitterly disassociated themselves from the church.

Late in 1969 the Hawks resigned and moved to Colorado. From the beginning of their tenure in Rimrock, Mrs. Hawk's enthusiasm for missionary work was never shared by her husband, nor had he ever taken an active part in local church activities. Mrs. Hawk worked very closely with the three Navajo congregations during her stay in Rimrock, and groups of the Indian members were frequent visitors in the missionary parsonage. One day, having tired of attempting to live under such "open-house" conditions, the distraught husband took a shotgun and quickly cleared the premises of the day's visitors, threatening further violence if they returned. Needless to say, the event had a fatal impact on the possibility of their further effectiveness in Rimrock.

From the fall of 1969 until the summer of 1970, the Rimrock Nazarenes were without missionary leadership. The lack of enthusiasm and the persistence of internal conflict over seemingly insignificant issues, coupled with the temporary absence of centralized authority, had a definitely weakening effect on the cohesiveness of the organization. This structural deficiency left the mission stations unprepared to cope with the advent of the Pentecostal movement into the area in the late spring of 1970.

Conflict and Factionalism (1969–1970)

The Church of God, Cleveland, Tennessee, had had a congregation under Navajo leadership at Rocky Point, New Mexico, since 1963. In the late fall of 1969 several Navajo members of the Nazarene mission in Rimrock, dissatisfied with the decline of emotionalism and the infrequency of "faith healings" in their own services, began to drive to the Pentecostal meetings in Rocky Point on Sundays. As a result of their interest, a young Church of God evangelist from Gallup, New Mexico, Billy Pino, began holding tent revivals in the Rimrock area during the following May.

The first meetings were held in a large tent erected adjacent to the Red Lake Nazarene Mission, and with few exceptions, participants were members of the Nazarene church. Emotionalism ran at a high pitch, many of the Navajos were reportedly healed, and the nightly services were a source of entertainment, even for those who came only to watch. Within a week, the group had moved out of the tent and into the Red Lake-mission facilities, despite the protests of the Nazarene leadership, where they held services for an additional week.

The majority of the Nazarene congregation was relatively unconcerned over the growing influence of the Pentecostal movement in Rimrock. Many of them had come in contact with the group before. Others were enjoying the spiritualism and enthusiasm. And regardless of their feelings about the new religious activity, most of them. with the exception of the native pastors and their families, saw no threat posed by the Pentecostal incursion. One of the converts to the new movement observed :

> Pentecosts say all the churches is good. The Nazarenes say the Pentecost is bad. Pentecost say you can go anywhere and pray, the Nazarene church, anywhere. The Bible is the same. They preach the same story. Everything's the same.

On the other hand, the Navajo leadership of the Nazarene-mission stations, their authority and income threatened by the Pentecostal successes, expressed grave concern over the presence of the new movement in Rimrock. Like the majority of their memberships, these local religious leaders had no quarrel with the new group over theological issues, but rather the practical matters relating to organizational structure and techniques. As Frank Chatto, one of the Nazarene pastors, put it

I stand for the Nazarene church to preach. I have authority to preach. I have a license to preach. I have redeemed my sermon. But I don't know about this Pentecost church. I just hear that you come to that church and you don't know where your offering goes. You don't know where your report goes. You just give the money. Maybe you just put it in your pocket. . . . We have a headquarters in Kansas City. This money goes there. . . . I'm not putting it in my pocket. Report goes to Superintendent Banks, how we operate this church, how many attendance do we have, and we have it every year, or every week. It's how they operate this church in the beginning. But I don't know about this Pentecost.

In June of 1970 the new missionaries, the Rockfords, arrived to take over the operation of the Rimrock work. Unlike his predecessors, Rockford was not an ordained clergyman. A former football coach and high-school principal, he considered himself more administrator than preacher. Similarly, less paternalistic toward the Navajos than those before him, Rockford took a hard-line position in dealing with missionary problems.

Although the Church of God evangelist had not been in the Rimrock area with his tent since May, in his absence factions had developed within the Nazarene-mission stations pitting the pro-Pentecostal element against those opposed to the movement. In spite of the new missionary's efforts to restore harmony, threats, personal attacks, accusations, and physical confrontations became expected procedure at mission services, especially at the Sand Mountain and Red Lake outposts. For this reason, when Billy Pino returned in late July, the situation was already on the verge of explosion.

With assistance from several local sympathizers, the young Pentecostal evangelist set up his operation in the vicinity of the Red Lake Mission for the second time, and within a few days had once again commandeered the Nazarene facilities. This brought a quick reaction from the missionary and district church authorities who moved immediately to have the intruding group removed from the premises by the Navajo police. To their dismay, however, they discovered that the Nazarenes had no more legal claim to the section of ground on which the church building stood than did the Church of God. The original lease agreement had only been a verbal contract with a Navajo couple that had since joined forces with the Pentecostal movement. Therefore, while the Nazarenes owned the building, the Penetecostals controlled the land. For the next few Sundays the Red Lake Nazarenes who had remained loyal to the older cause were forced to hold services in the home of one of the members.

By the time the Pentecostal evangelist closed the July revival, both sides of the local controversy had developed such hostilities that reconciliation appeared impossible. Nazarene loyalists demanded that the Pentecostal enthusiasts abandon their recently acquired habits, such as clapping in church, or be refused reentry into the mission organization. On the other hand, the splinter group, rather than renounce their new faith, began to hold services in private homes and make plans to organize a Rimrock Church of God.

The Pentecostals staged another revival in Rimrock, late in September of 1970. This time they moved into the area of the Sand Mountain Nazarene Mission where the former assistant pastor and his wife had recently left the church in protest over his failure to be reelected. Setting up the large tent and a public-address system that amplified and projected the sound for several miles in all directions, the Rev. Pino and his assistants conducted a two-week meeting. The nightly services attracted from seventy-fie to a hundred of the Rimrock Navajos. The great majority of the participants were women and children. Of the men who attended, most sat in back rows and merely observed. Singing and clapping to the accompaniment of guitar, drums, trumpet, and organ, the crowds became almost frantically emotional. A number of "miraculous" experiences were reported, but according to the evangelist himself, no one "received the gift of tongues" during any of the Rimrock revival services.

Following the September meetings, allegiance among the Rimrock Navajos were fairly well defined. Hostilities between the two groups—Pentecostal and Nazarenes—continued, there was some active intersect proselyting attempts, and rumors were occasionally circulated about some new atrocity, such as human sacrifice, being committed in the Pentecostal services, but the majority of the local church population was resolved to the fact that the new movement was in Rimrock to stay.

Attendance at the mission stations had fallen drastically by at the end of the year, and the Nazarene leadership continued to express great amazement over the fact that the Church of God had cut so quickly and sharply into their numbers. Some blamed it on the appeal of the Pentecostal activities to the "baser" motives inherent in traditional Navajo religion. Frank Chatto argued :

> I know the Pentecostal church. I went two times, three times. ... The preacher preached, called those to the front that wanted healing. He put his hands on their heads. They start to dance around. Some started to dance and they shake and they fall down. There was lots of noise. Big drums was drumming. . . . Some of the people they fall, almost on you. . . . It looks like this world religion. I know some of my old religion, the Navajo religion; they used to do that all the time.

Mrs. Myrtle Apachio, one of the Navajos remaining loyal to the Nazarene cause, correlated the Pentecostal experience and traditional hand-trembling patterns :

> In the Navajo traditional way, they predict things through their hands. They put their hands and they shake them a little bit, and when they get through, sometimes they throw things on the ground. This will tell a sick person what his problem is. They get together in a hogan and they work their hands. The hands draw a pattern or touch you and tell you what's wrong with you. This is the way they tell this sick person that he is sick and why he is sick; because someone is thinking bad of him or something.
> We went and when we got over there [the Pentecostal revival], there were people there that I'd never seen before. They all had great big instruments and rattles . . . things to make noise with. They said they were going to pray just after we got there, and they started shaking their hands like they did in the old way, the old time. . . . I got scared.

The Nazarene missionary, slow to atempt to explain the phenomenon, did spend many hours puzzling over the blow dealt his group by the crusading Pentecostals:

> How can the Lord bless that kind of thing? They come right in and proselyte right under our noses, right next to our churches. That's an ethical issue. That's ruthless. How can the Lord bless that kind of thing? Of course, the devil has some power. . . . How come the Navajo don't see all the things the Nazarenes have done for them? It seems to me that a person would have to appreciate a work that's been here for twenty-seven years and been solid and stood by them. We've done a lot for them, and they know it. . . . I guess we'll know in heaven who's been right.

With the polarization of the two groups, certain structural observations have been made possible. In the first place, church allegiance falls very clearly along kinship lines. Generally speaking, while not all members may attend with regularity, when one individual in an extended family or unit expresses a preference for either Nazarenism or Pentecostalism, the remaining persons will admit to a similar sentiment. This does not necessarily hold true at the group or outfit level. Again, similar to Walker's Nez Perce Pentecostal faction, Church of God converts in Rimrock tend to have less education, smaller incomes, and are generally less acculturated than members of the older, more established organization.[18]

Stagnation (1971– ?)

Early 1971 found the Nazarene mission among the Rimrock Navajos reeling from the setback at the hands of the Pentecostal faction and still suffering from a variety of internal problems. There were groups within the church who continued to debate over what their attitude should be toward the Pentecostal people in the community. Attacks on the character and ability of the Navajo pastors and the missionary, and a general lack of concern among the membership in the area of organizational responsibilities also helped to further weaken the overall program of the Nazarenes. As a result, attendance levels were suffering.

In the spring of 1971 many of the more established communicants of the Nazarene Church in Rimrock were expressing concern over the future of their organization. It appeared to many of them the problems and lagging attendance were predicting a slow death for the local mission. No one seemed to care anymore, and no one seemed to know why. Long-time church member, Charles Yazi, explained the situation :

> We preach pretty strict; hard. We tell them not to have stealing or do any adultery. Don't tell lies or story, or marry some other woman and let the children go. . . . But the main thing we ask is tithe. . . . We tell them to give. Give back to God whatever he give you. . . . That's what's tough for them. . . . So it seems pretty tough for them to come to church. . . . The first time Brother Fry come, all the people come. Slowly and gradually they pass away. Now it isn't much. Just the old religion, the old Christians. They come alone, with just the children. The old women. . . . It makes it pretty tough on the young people to believe.

It was obvious that the attitude of the Nazarene missionaries themselves had come a long way since the days of Fry and his blind optimism. Rockford once complained :

> You can't depend on the Navajo for anything. You get them to teach a class or go pick up children for Sunday School, and they hardly ever show up. Even the best of them aren't dependable. I don't know if it's worth it. I don't think these people will ever change. Everyone has always let them do anything they've wanted to do, and as a result, now they can't accept any kind of responsibility.

In the spring of 1972 a discouraged Rockford and his family resigned and went back to Texas. His replacement, Harold Hunter, was a small, middle-aged preacher from Oklahoma who saw himself committed to Indian young people. In his own words :

> It doesn't make sense to worry about the old Navajos anymore. I don't think they understand what it's all about. They

come and participate, but I really wonder. . . . It's the young people. We've got to get to the young people if we expect to do any good out here.

Because of his soft-spoken and unaggressive approach Hunter has been able to avoid much of the opposition encountered by Rockford, but the general apathy among Nazarenes in the area was still evident in the summer of 1973.

The future of the Church of the Nazarene in Rimrock is uncertain, but it is doubtful that they will ever again attain the power and influence they exercised during the second phase of their history in the Navajo community.

THE MORMON MISSION

The first Anglo settlers in the Rimrock area were the Mormon missionaries, but their proselyting activities were soon abandoned, once the problem of survival became a full-time occupation for the Saints. It was not until the 1940s that any concerted effort was made again to convert the Navajos, but despite the renewed missionary concern and the establishment of a Lamanite branch of the local ward, Mormonism has had a minimal impact on the lives of the Rimrock Navajos.

Background

The Church of Jesus Christ and the Latter Day Saints was organized in the 1830s by Joseph Smith, the original prophet through whom God revealed the sacred *Book of Mormon*.[19] Denying any connections with Protestantism, the Saints claim to have recaptured the spirit of the true church of Christ, an organization historically defunct in the West from the time of Constantine in the fourth century A.D. up until the birth of Mormonism. With a well-run and tightly knit institutional machinery and heaquarters in Salt Lake City, the L.D.S. church has a world membership of approximately three million.

The theological premises that govern Mormon life are best expressed in thirteen "Articles of Faith." These include belief statements affirming the existence of God, the divinity of Jesus, the reality of individual sin, the significance of baptism, the verbal inerrancy of the Bible and the *Book of Mormon,* the sanctity of law, and the ultimate right of religious freedom.[20]

In actual practice, the two most important virtues in Mormonism appear to be belief and ethical behavior. By the former is meant rational assent to the proposition that the L.D.S. church is the only "true" church and that the *Book of Mormon* is the revealed word of God, and by the latter is intended the abstinence of all "strong drink" : alcoholic beverages, coffee, and tea.

Despite the apparent stringency of "article" stipulations, the Mormons have never made any explicit theological demands on their Navajo converts beyond the condition that they believe in the historicity of the *Book of Mormon* and observe the "strong drink" restrictions. While they have not been necessarily encouraged by the Saints to do so, Rimrock-Navajo members of the L.D.S. organization have always felt free to maintain and practice their customary ceremonies.

Unlike the Nazarenes, who demand that the Indians aspiring to membership denounce the essential ideological and practical elements of Navajo traditional religious life, the Mormons feel that the process of actually becoming a Latter Day Saint is an extended, educative one, considerably more involved than a simple, immediate act, such as conversion or baptism. Most Rimrock Mormons contend that the Navajos who are baptized very rarely, if ever, understand the significance of this most vital of sacraments, and therefore they do not expect radical change. In light of this, the majority of the Rimrock Navajos have never felt their traditional life-styles threatened by the tenets of Mormonism and make a very clear distinction between the demands of the two missionary programs operative in the area. Typically, one older Navajo recently testified :

I joined the Mormon church three years ago and I still believe in the old way (*'aal'kidááyaa k'ehgo*). . . . the Mormons say they believe in the Navajo ways, but the Nazarenes say they don't. When they get sick they just send them to the hospital.

Ritual demands placed on Navajo converts by the Mormons are also minimal. The only absolute requirement is that they be baptized, by immersion, and allow their names to be placed on the church rolls. While it is not made mandatory, the Rimrock Navajos are encouraged to have their marriages solemnized in the church and, if sufficient genealogical information is available, submit to "baptism for the dead." This latter sacrament is a means whereby Mormons may insure the afterlife status of their ancestors who have passed on, not having had the opportunity as mortals to establish their sainthood. Some of the Rimrock-Navajo communicants report having traveled to the Mormon temple in Mesa, Arizona, where they were baptized as many as twenty-five times, vicariously observing the rite for as many deceased kinfolk.

Rationale

The focus of Mormon-missionary concern has always been the American Indian. According to L.D.S. tradition:

The Lamanites, while increasing in numbers, fell under the curse of divine displeasure; they became dark in skin and benighted in spirit, forgot the God of their fathers, lived in a wild nomadic life, and degenerated into the fallen state in which the American Indians—their lineal descendants—were found by those who rediscovered the western continent in latter times.[21]

The responsibility of the Latter Day Saints to these "degenerate" peoples is clearly indicated in the *Book of Mormon* (2, Nephi, 30:5–6):

And the gospel of Jesus Christ shall be declared among them the Indians, wherefore, they shall be restored unto the knowledge of their fathers, and also to the knowledge of Jesus Christ, which was had among their fathers.

And then shall they rejoice; for they shall know that it is a blessing unto them from the hand of God; and their scales of darkness shall begin to fall from their eyes; and many generations shall not pass away among them, save they shall be a white and delightsome people.

Early History

The first Mormon attempts to proselyte among the Indians of the American Southwest were initiated in the 1850s under the direction of Brigham Young. Extended forays into southern Utah and northern Arizona brought the missionary groups into contact first with the Utes and the Hopi. Under instructions from church authorities, the missionaries attempted to familiarize themselves with the particular language, present the *Book of Mormon* to the Lamanites as the true and revealed history of the American Indians, and teach the principles of the Gospel.

During their work with the Hopi and the Utes covering the next ten years, from about 1860 to 1870, the Mormons occasionally came into contact with isolated groups of Navajos. Incidents of open conflict between Mormons and Navajos in this period led to a confrontation at Fort Defiance in 1870 and an attempt to establish peace. Despite the subsequent improvement of relations between the two factions, it was not until 1875 that the first Navajo was baptized by the Saints.

With the establishment of the Little Colorado communities in the 1870s, Brigham Young gave specific instructions to the settlers as to their missionary responsibilities:

We desire that the settlements in the Little Colorado be built up to the Lord in righteousness, wherein an example will be set to the surrounding tribes of the Lamanites, and indeed to all others of the way the Lord will build up Zion. . . . Treat them with kindness . . . set a proper example. . . . Instruct them in the Gospel. . . . Teach them to live in peace, become free from native vices, and become useful citizens in the Kingdom . . .

(Letter to the elders of the Little Colorado settlements from Brigham Young).[22]

As the Mormons began to move in and settle the Rimrock area, they made definite efforts to fulfill their missionary obligations, and by 1877 thirty-four Navajos had been baptized.[23] Nonetheless, the matter of gaining a livelihood soon replaced missionizing concerns so thoroughly that, for all practical purposes, proselyting was abandoned in Rimrock after December 1877.[24]

The Rimrock Mormons were officially released from the missionary responsibilities in 1900, but even after this the impulse to convert the Lamanites continued to make its presence felt. "Some of the Saints still heard the call to labor among the Indians. . . . The missionary duty was not forgotten."[25]

The acting bishop expressed concern in 1904 that the Lamanites "come to the understanding of the gospel and be educated and brought out of their benighted conditions."[26] That same year, though, "when some of the Indians wanted to bury their dead in the community cemetery, they were considered 'outsiders' rather than 'brethren.' "[27]

With the passage of time, the responsibilities felt by the Mormons toward the Rimrock Navajos became more generalized. As expressed by one of the Saints in 1922: "We should try and help our Indian neighbors by being good neighbors. Show them what is wrong and which is right."[28] Aaron Cox, an older Mormon, expressed a similar attitude as late as 1970: "I've worked and slept side by side with the 'Navviehos' and always have tried to set a good example and show them there's a better way."

Recent History

In the years following World War II the Mormons once again attempted to renew and revamp missionary efforts among the Indians in the Southwest. The revitalization of the general program, coupled with the recent advent of the Nazarenes on the Rimrock scene, brought a new missionary spirit to the local ward.

In 1949 the Southwest Indian Mission was created by the Mormon church. Under the new department, services to the Lamanites were to be broadened. Religious-instruction classes and relief societies were to be organized, and practical help in the household arts was to be rendered.

That same year (1949) work was begun on a Mormon-Indian chapel near the chapter house in Rimrock. The following October the chapel was dedicated, and the ward clerk reported a total of 257 Lamanite members on the new church rolls.

Rapoport labeled this phase (1946–1950) of Mormon activities among the Navajo in Rimrock, "The Period of Mission Revitalization," and in light of recent developments predicted: there is a good likelihood that the Mormon mission . . . will have a certain success.[29]

Over the next twenty years, however, despite a separate chapel, the frequent efforts of outside missionaries and local-ward personnel and a program that functioned with some regularity, Mormon accomplishments among the Rimrock Navajos were minimal. Attendance at the Sunday services of the Indian church rarely exceeded thirty in the years between 1950 and 1970 except on special occasions. Reportedly, only one of the Navajo Mormons was a regular tither, and annual income at the chapel ran less than two hundred dollars annually,

During the years that the Indian chapel functioned, weekly attendance was generally composed of members of four or five regular families, three of which belonged to the same outfit.

On several occasions in the 1950s, missionary conferences were held in the Rimrock area. Such events were attempts to encourage increased participation in church activities by the Navajos and to revitalize the missionizing efforts of the local Anglo Saints. Conducted by outsiders, the conferences appear to have had little effect on Navajo attendance or attitudes among white ward members.

Also during the fifties, the general church began to send more elders into the area on assignment. These workers, usually young college-age men on a two-year mission with the L.D.S. church, operated under the direct auspices of the Southwest Indian Mission. Visiting in the homes of the Navajos, praying, teaching, and encouraging nonmembers to be baptized, the elders, because of the fact that they were generally perceived as outsiders, were more readily accepted than the local part-time missionaries. Between 1957 and 1959, sixty-four Rimrock Navajos were baptized by the elders in special services conducted at the Rimrock Reservoir. In spite of the growing membership rolls during this period, atendance at the regular services of the Indian chapel remainder relatively unchanged.

In 1961 the first Navajo men from the Rimrock area assumed roles as Mormon elders and went on a two-year mission for the church. That same year the Indian chapel was closed for almost fourteen months because of a general lack of interest among Navajos and Anglos alike. During the period of discontinued operations, Navajo members were encouraged to attend the services at the ward sanctuary in the Rimrock village, but actual Indian attendance was slight.

In 1962 the Rimrock Ward Indian Branch was reorganized as the El Morro Branch. In addition to the regular Sunday service, a Sunday-school program was added "for the Lamanite members in our ward so they might have more chance to participate."[30]

In 1964 the branch was closed again for several months. The chapel was reopened in 1965 as the Rimrock First Branch. Over the next five years, operations at the chapel were very erratic. New missionaries, novel programs, and fresh ward enthusiasm often sparked activities at the Indian branch, but most of the interest was short-lived.

Finally, in March of 1970, ward leaders admitted the failure and general unproductiveness of the sporadic program at the Indian chapel, and the Rimrock Ward and Rimrock Branch were officially merged. Justification for the discontinuation of a separate Indian organization by the Mormons in the Rimrock area has been expressed as a desire to integrate in a common fellowship involving both Anglos and Navajos.

The Program in 1970

By the end of 1970 the locally directed Mormon-missionary program in Rimrock had, with few exceptions, been abandoned. Those Indians so desiring were free to attend the ward services where they were provided space for their own Sunday-school class and given the opportunity to testify in the monthly "Sacrament and Testimony" meeting. Actual Navajo attendance averaged less than twelve persons per week and usually included the same group of regulars: the Sunday-school instructor, Juan Begay, and his family, plus an elderly man, and two middle-aged women.

Local Mormons continued to operate the Mutual Improvement Association (M.I.A.) and seminary program for the Navajo children living at the dormitory. These organizations, under the direction of the only salaried church official in the Rimrock ward, met every Tuesday and Thursday evening, respectively, and provided doctrinal instruction and entertainment for those Indian children whose parents had requested that they participate. Similar to and simultaneous with the Nazarene "youth-training program," these functions provided natural opportunities for systematic religious instruction.

Outside elders continued to spend short periods of time working among the Rimrock Navajos in 1970. Seven years prior to this the Mormon church had initiated a concentrated, ten-week language course for its young men preparing for a mission, and with varying degrees of proficiency, the elders could handle at least minimal amounts of Navajo conversation. This ability made a favorable impression on the Navajos and gave the missionaries additional opportunities to deliver their message. Carrying a portable tape recorder and a film-strip projector, they visited hogans throughout the area, teaching by means of their mechanical equipment and encouraging the Navajos to get involved in the regular activities of the ward.

With its limited and irregular schedule, the missionary program of the Mormons among the Rimrock Navajos had, by 1970, lost most of its enthusiasm and vitality that had portended institutional success in the fall of 1950, and this continued to be the case by mid-1973.

The L.D.S. Church in Rimrock.

Problems

Because the Mormons in Rimrock have never escaped, from the Indian perspective, their image as land-grabbers and exploiters, it is ironic that they should even attempt to convert the local Navajos. However, despite the distrust and bitterness persisting in the Navajo-Mormon relationship, the Saints have been able to solicit at least token allegiance from several hundred of The People in the area.

Many of the Rimrock Mormons have grown quite pessimistic about the significance of mission work among the Navajos. Accusing the Indians of being purely opportunistic in their religious decisions, they point to the situations in the past where Navajo response has been predicated wholly on the expectation of material return. For example, in 1959 a Christmas service was held at the Indian chapel, in place of the regular Sunday-morning program. Dinner was served, treats were distributed, and gifts were passed out following the worship service. On this occasion, 290 Navajos were present, whereas attendance on the Sundays immediately before and after totaled ten and one, respectively.

Because of the limited demands placed on the Navajo converts by the L.D.S. missionaries and the irregularity of the Lamanite program in the Rimrock area, defining what is meant by a Mormon Navajo is very difficult. As Rapoport observed several years ago: "The Mormon group shades off imperceptibly into the main Navajo non-Christian population."[31] As I was forced to admit in the selection of my sample, the only way to meaningfully separate the Mormon Navajos from the traditionals is by looking at their overall attendance record, and, the crowded membership rolls notwithstanding, very few meet even minimum qualifying standards. Many of those who have been baptized openly admit that they have never once attended an L.D.S. function.

Some of the factors underlying what success they have had also help to explain the general failure of the Mormon-missionary work among the Rimrock Navajos. The flexibility of doctrinal demands, the impersonal nature of ties between the Navajos and outside missionaries, and direct appeal to material needs in the proselyting encounter, while they expedite initial decision, militate against the development of permanent commitments.

Many of the causes behind the difficulties of the Rimrock-ward missionary program are the direct responsibilty of the local membership. The declining interest in the Lamanite work and the irregularity of the Indian services and activities have discouraged many of the Navajos who have grown to expect an uncertainty in their relationship with the church. Elders visiting in the Rimrock ward often critically observe that local members are more complacent and less enthusiastic about the Lamanite mission than Mormons elsewhere in the Southwest. They claim that Rimrock Mormons are still not willing to accept the notion of Indian equality or the responsibility of "fellowshipping" on a one-to-one basis with the Navajos. It is their contention that without this type of interaction, mission work will never succeed.

Whatever the reasons, it is obvious that the Mormons, despite their occasional emphases and the frequency of visiting missionaries, have had a relatively insignificant impact on the religious lives of the Rimrock Navajo.

NAZARENE-MORMON RELATIONS

When the Nazarenes first brought their missionary operation to Rimrock in 1944, the Mormons, by nature inclined toward a religious exclusivism, were surprisingly tolerant.

Attitudes began to change, though, as the new missionary, the Rev. Fry, began to get more involved in community affairs. In the first place, he tried to institute religious instruction in the schools, and the Mormons, in line with their explicit separation of church functions and public education, reacted strongly. Again, in an attempt to disassociate himself from Mormon missionary efforts and their inherent liabilities, Fry increasingly reinforced the historical distinctiveness between Nazarenism and Mormonism. In this context he made it quite clear that Nazarenes, unlike the Mormons, had never stolen the Navajo's land, shot their animals, or cheated them over a trading counter. In short, it soon became evident to local Mormons that perhaps there was room for only one missionary operation in the area, and with the revitalization of their program, interdenominational hostilities began to materialize.

The Nazarene missionary that came to Rimrock in 1950 was less vociferous and controversial by nature than had been his immediate predecessor, and during his term antagonistic attitudes were mollified. Banks displayed an interest in community affairs, participating in village activities, donating labor in the construction of the new high school, and developing friendships with local Mormons. As a result of his openness and personal involvement, members of the Rimrock ward began to emphasize the commonalities of Mormonism and the Nazarene cause, and the new mission became less of a direct threat to the Saints.

By 1973 very little ill-feeling persisted in the relationship between the two groups at all. With the exception of an occasional testimony in which a Navajo would defend the relative superiority of his church as opposed to the other, there were very few even hints of friction. The Mormons, because of the inactivity of their own missionary program, were very quick to admit that the Nazarenes had been "doing a better job with the Navajos."

The new intergroup goodwill also had some of its roots in several recent historical events affecting the whole community. In the first place, since the Nazarenes had moved their main operation to the outskirts of the Rimrock village, they had taken a more active role in local affairs and had got more personally involved with the Anglo Mormons. Again, because of the pressures being placed on the white element in Rimrock by the militant faction in the new Navajo high school, the Nazarene missionaries, older Indian members of both groups, and the white Saints had become part of a common reactionary force.

THE GENERAL RELIGIOUS SITUATION (1973)

From a statistical perspective, the situation in Rimrock, as of August 1973, reflected a surprisingly even distribution in

Navajo religious affiliations. In terms of membership rolls, there were approximately 375 Nazarenes, 265 Mormons, twenty-five Pentecostals, twenty-five other denominations, with the remaining 450 falling under the general rubric of traditional. However, in terms of actual participation, there were approximately 200 Nazarenes, 125 Pentecostals, and twenty Mormons, with the others (900) being classed in a catchall *other* or *traditional* category. This is in comparison to statistics for 1950 that show approximately eighty Nazarenes and twenty-five Mormons actively involved in the respective missions.

In reality, the Rimrock-Navajo population represents a broad spectrum of religious behavior and ideological orientations. Any statistical groupings are thus more or less artificial and do not ultimately reflect any hard-and-fast distinctions, either behaviorally or ideologically.

However, my primary assumption is that if a Navajo has participated in a specific form of Christian religious activity with any consistency over a twenty-year period, it is likely that he has developed some unique attitudes and behavior characteristics that set him apart from members of other groups, be they Western or traditional. Therefore, recognizing that the two to three decades of Rimrock history have been in part defined by the activities of only three distinct types of religious orientations, it is legitimate, for purposes of analyzing the economic correlates of ideological change, to divide the Rimrock Navajos into three basic categories: Nazarenes, Mormon, and traditional.

Assuming, then, that the historical participation factor is a sufficient criterion for subdividing the Rimrock-Navajo religious populations, despite the recent intrusion of a new phenomenon that has altered some patterns in the area, a further step is justified. Since the primary concern in this study is the nature of the influence exerted by Christian ideology and mission techniques on economic behavior, it is necessary, in many cases, that the Nazarene and Mormon memberships be grouped into one category. At this point, they can then be treated in the Rimrock situation in terms of two general religious groups:

those who have participated in the activities of the Christian missions over the past twenty years and those who have not. In the sampling procedure, the criteria have been much more demanding, so that in the actual analysis, the two groups with which I am dealing are, on the one hand, those who have attended mission services with some degree of regularity in the period since the early fifties and, on the other hand, those who have remained faithful to traditional religious commitments during this period. In the end, I am thus left with a basic dichotomy that can be characterized in several ways: churched and nonchurched; Christian and non-Christian; modern and traditional.

In my observations of the Rimrock situation, at no time did I encounter a Navajo who claimed to have *no* religious faith. Either he would confess to belonging to a particular denomination or would affirm his commitment to Navajo ideology. Even those among the educated Navajos who had been through the acceptance-rejection cycle in a particular Christian organization, did not take a nonbeliever's position on the religious issue. Rather they were quite explicit in admitting their unabashed allegiance to traditional Navajo religion.

The last few years in Rimrock have seen a flurry of traditional ceremonies and group activities. In the early fall of 1970 and midsummers of 1972 and 1973 Enemy Way squaw dances were conducted for the benefit of Korean War veterans. In the spring of 1971 Juan Begay, often referred to by local Anglos as "the most stable Navajo member of the Mormon Ward," held an expensive, four-day sing in an attempt to correct a persistent back ailment.

Fear of witchcraft is still a common emotion in Rimrock and in recent years there have been many reports of the phenomenon. Many of the Navajos continue to explain misfortune—sickness, dead sheep, and bad weather—by reference to specific incidents and personal sources of witchery.

Regardless of the continuing importance attached to traditional religious values, the prevailing atmosphere at most public gatherings among the Rimrock Navajos is very Christian. The Rimrock-Navajo Rodeo, school functions, and other group activities are always opened with prayer, and the great majority of the Navajos present stand with heads bowed and eyes closed. Again, the handshake, a custom introduced by Mormon missionaries, has become almost instinctive among the Navajos, and the average conversation, especially between Anglo and Indian, is often characterized by Christian symbols and biblical illustrations.

The future of the Christian religion among the Rimrock Navajos remains an open question. It is unlikely that the Mormons will ever develop a more effective program, and it would also appear that the Nazarenes have reached a plateau in terms of their total growth potential. On the other hand, the Pentecostal group may well hold the key to Rimrock's religious future. If they realize their expressed intentions of organizing a local church and offering a full program, they could easily involve a large proportion of the Navajo community within the next five years. Nonetheless, acculturation in the area is portending a unique mixture of traditionalism and secularity that might spell disaster for all three of the programs.

NOTES

1. Quoted by Robert W. Young, *The Navajo Yearbook* (Window Rock, Arizona: Navajo Agency, 1961), p. 511.

2. Clyde Kluckhohn and Dorothea C. Leighton, *The Navajo*, rev. ed. (Garden City, New York: Doubleday), p. 225. For a comprehensive analysis of traditional Navajo religion, *see* Gladys Reichard, *Navajo Religion* (New York: Bollingen Foundation, 1950); Leland C. Wyman, "The Religion of the Navajo Indians," in *Ancient Religions*, ed Vergilius Ferm (New York: Citadel Press, 1950), pp. 343–61.

3. Kluckhohn, "The Rimrock Navajo," p. 371.

4. Church of the Nazarene, *Voice of the Redman*, January 1959 (Kansas City, Missouri: Nazarene Publishing House), p. 2.

5. Rapoport, p. 22.

6. Church of the Nazarene, *Voice of the Redman*, December 1955, p. 4.

7. Rapoport, pp. 16–35.

8. Ibid.

9. Ibid., p. 17.

10. Ibid., p. 21.

11. Ibid., p. 22.

12. Ibid., p. 28.

13. Ibid., p. 31.

14. Ibid., p. 32.

15. Ibid., p. 35.

16. Traditionally, Athabascans, which include both Navajos and Apaches, have had a tremendous fear of the dead.

17. Church of the Nazarene, "District Assembly Minutes, North American Indian District" (Kansas City, Missouri: Nazarene Publishing House, 1960), p. 21.

18. Deward Walker, *Conflict and Schism in Nez Perce Acculturation* (Pullman, Washington: Washington State University, 1968), p. 98.

19. For a thorough discussion of Mormon history and doctrine, *see* Thomas F. O'Dea, *The Mormons* (Chicago: University of Chicago Press, 1957).

20. James E. Talmadge, *A Study of the Articles of Faith* (Salt Lake City: Deseret Book Company, 1924), pp. 1–3.

21. Ibid., p. 260.

22. Quoted by David Kay Flake, "A History of Mormon Missionary Work with the Hopi, Navajo, and Zuni Indians" (Masters thesis, Brigham Young University, 1965), p. 57.

23. Telling, p. 2.

24. Flake, p. 71.

25. Telling, p. 45.

26. Rimrock Ward Historical Record, unpublished documents (Rimrock, New Mexico: Church of Jesus Christ of Latter Day Saints, 1904).

27. Telling, p. 45.

28. Rimrock Ward Historical Record, 1922.

29. Rapoport, p. 43.

30. Rimrock Ward Indian Branch Historical Record, unpublished documents (Rimrock, New Mexico: Church of Jesus Christ of Latter Day Saints, 1962).

31. Rimrock Files, 10 August 1950, p. 3.

Signs of change in Rimrock.

3

The Dollars and Cents
of Sainthood

As noted earlier, the Navajo economic base has undergone several critical transformations in the course of The People's history in the Southwest. The most recent of these changes has been the increasing involvement in the cash-wage economy of the twentieth century. By 1970 the Rimrock Navajos had begun to participate directly in the Western capitalistic system. In this process the "churched" faction of the community appeared to be making a much more effective adjustment than did the traditional group.

In this chapter I describe the Rimrock-Navajo economy, the basic changes of recent years, and, comparatively, the extent to which my three groups are developing modern patterns of economic rationality.

Much of the land is completely unarable.

The desolate area south of town.

Land

Essential to traditional Navajo economic enterprises is the availability of sufficient quantities of land with at least minimal support capacities. Because of the nature of the soils and terrain in the Rimrock area, grazing and dry farming require large outlays of land even for small agricultural operations. Thus, despite the fact that the Indians now control about 125 acres of land per individual, the value of that total, in terms of actual potential, is relatively insignificant.

In 1950 the Rimrock Navajos controlled 153,600 acres. Of that total, 1,085 were used for dry farming, while 126,350 were committed to grazing purposes.[1] By 1970 that total had risen only slightly to 154,100 acres. Of this land, twenty-six percent was individually owned or allotted, thirty-eight percent was owned by the tribe, and thirty-six percent was leased from the state. That same year 142,600 acres were used for grazing and about 800 for dry farming.

Traditionally, the Navajos have always been extremely flexible in matters involving land rights and ownership. Pasture and water were seen as belonging to everyone, and controls were limited.

The Rimrock Navajos have learned, in direct confrontations with Anglos, that open grazing is not profitable and that land rights must be treated as permanent. Mormon ranchers in the Rimrock area have reportedly shot Navajo livestock that accidentally wandered onto their ranges. Again, the Navajos have often complained about Mormon cattle destroying large portions of their cultivated crops. Despite traditional inclinations to the contrary, more and more of the Navajos have begun to construct fences around their allotments and openly defend personal-property rights, not only in disputes with whites, but also among themselves.

ECONOMIC ENTERPRISES AND SOURCES OF INCOME

Hunting and Gathering

The oldest economic activity of significance in Rimrock is hunting and gathering. Various game animals are hunted and eaten, plants are collected for medicinal and food purposes, wood is gathered for fuel and dwelling construction, and pinyon nuts are collected for sale.

It has been shown that between the 1870s and the 1940s there was a significant decline in the numbers of larger, wild animal life in the Rimrock area, so that there was not "a sufficient quantity in 1941 to provide any regular percentage of local food incomes."[2] The loss has been blamed on destructive hunting, heavy stock grazing, and fence construction.

By 1950 the role of wildlife in the composition of the Rimrock-Navajo diet was minimal. Some rabbits, porcupines, and deer were occasionally used, but birds were almost never eaten, in most cases because of ritual taboo.

The hunting enterprise had changed little in the Rimrock area by 1970. The Navajos shot and ate several deer, both in and out of season. They also took advantage of available small game: rabbits, porcupines, and prairie dogs. While most adults denied it, some of the Navajo children admitted to having eaten skunk. Overall, however, edible wild animal life was scarce, with the exception of the rabbits and prairie dogs, and added little to the process of sustaining human life in Rimrock.

Gathering activities have long served crucial functions in the lives of the Rimrock Navajos. The dependency on wood has made its collection an almost daily routine, especially in the winter months. The quest for available firewood and building timbers was once a source of friction between the Mormons and The People, but by 1970 there were sufficient supplies and fewer demands by whites, so that the activity did not present the same problems. In fact, the Rimrock area had developed a reputation for its plentiful supply of fuel wood. Navajos from various parts of the Reservation had been known to drive for several hundred miles to take advantage of Rimrock's natural abundance.

While plants, such as yucca, were still gathered for ceremonial, medicinal, and cosmetic purposes in 1970, the activity involved only the more traditional Navajos. A few tubers, seeds, and fruits were also collected and eaten.

Economically speaking, the most important item gathered by the Rimrock Navajos has long been the pinyon nut. Generally, prime yields occur in seven-year intervals, and, in these years, local incomes are significantly effected. Collecting the nuts by picking directly from the trees or by robbing rats' nests, the Navajos sacked and sold almost $18,000 worth of the pinyons in 1936. In that year, this represented about ten percent of their total income.

The most recent pinyon year in Rimrock was 1969. During that fall, the local trader bought 44,000 pounds at sixty cents a pound—compared to twenty cents a pound in 1949—paying out a total of almost $27,000 to the gatherers.

Animal Husbandry

Sheep and Goats

Livestock raising, a Navajo occupation for more than 200 years, has been a way of life with the Rimrock group since they first settled in the area. The principal grazing animal has always been the sheep. In the early years following resettlement, the Rimrock Navajos were given a large herd of sheep by the government. These were soon crossbred with animals obtained from area Spanish-Americans. The latter also instructed the Navajos in improved methods of animal husbandry.

The breed of animals that eventually developed was a hardy cross between the Spanish-American Rambouillet and the smaller, tougher Navajo sheep. Though yielding less wool, these animals were considered "good stock for the country."[3] Still, Navajo sheep average only six pounds of wool annually, and fifty-seven lambs per 100 ewes are all that survive. This is in comparison to similar figures of eight and seventy, respectively, for Anglo sheep in the area.

The advent of government stock reduction in the 1930s had a dramatic impact on the Rimrock-Navajo economy and, expectedly, the pattern of livestock holdings in the area has changed. In the first place, sheep totals have diminished with fewer families owning a greater percentage of the animals. Again, the number of cows and horses has increased noticeably, relative to sheep and goat figures. In 1951 the Rimrock Navajos owned 7,318 sheep and 580 goats, besides 199 cows and 460 horses. By 1970 there were 6,700 sheep, 1,196 goats, 485 cows, and 422 horses.

In 1951, forty-four percent of the family units among the Rimrock Navajos owned no sheep, and one of the units controlled nine percent of all the sheep in the area. By 1970, sixty percent had no sheep and forty-five percent of all the animals were owned by ten families. That same year, the largest herd was comprised of 574 sheep and goats, while the smallest boasted a total of only three animals. Still, the trend has generally been toward more flocks and fewer animals.

In recent years grazing activities have been on a decline in the Rimrock area. There are several factors that account for this situation. The most direct explanation lies in the fact that the livestock enterprise has become continually uneconomical for the Navajos. The weather has been a major factor, because drought conditions have limited the grazing potential of range areas. Improper animal-husbandry practices have also had a constricting effect on wool and lamb production. Navajos often herd on horseback, and the sheep may be left in the same grazing spot for long periods of time or in the corral during the heat of the day. Such practices are detrimental to the health and general quality of the animals.

Another element discouraging the growth of the local sheep and wool industry is the hard work involved in the annual cycle of raising livestock. Charles Yazi has complained:

It's pretty tough to make a living on sheep. Pretty tough. No matter how hot it is, you have to follow them. No matter how much it is cold, the wind blowing, the snow blowing, you have to follow them. You can't turn them loose. If we just turn them loose a coyote come and get them; some man come and steal them. We got to watch them pretty close.

The annual grazing cycle itself begins in winter for the Rimrock Navajos. During the days of late November and early December the ewes, wethers, and lambs are brought together with the bucks, and the breeding season begins. Winter is an inopportune time for open-range grazing, and most sheepmen must supplement available forage with corn cake and alfalfa. After a breeding season of a few weeks, the bucks are separated from the other sheep, usually in late December.

The next important event is the lambing season, late in the month of April. The lambing ewes are separated from the rest of the flock, and within a few weeks the lambs are born. Out of a flock of 100, according to Navajo ranchers, the yield should be about eighty lambs. Within a few weeks after their birth, most of the male lambs are castrated, in the attempt to fatten them for the fall market. Because it occurs simultaneously with the cultivating and planting, lambing season is the busiest period of the year for the traditional Rimrock Navajos.

Shearing takes place in the middle of June. The wool, in 1970, was still being clipped with mechanical shears and, for most outfits in the area, it was a cooperative enterprise, with their most talented shearers bearing the brunt of the responsibility. Some of the Navajos, however, hired "experts" to handle the process. After the wool is clipped, it is packaged in 200-pound sacks and stored until the last sheep has been shorn. Then it is taken to the trading post where it is weighed and purchased by the trader.

In 1970 the Rimrock Navajos sold 30,941 pounds of wool at twenty-eight cents a pound for a total of almost $8,500. (This figure includes cash from the sale of a few pounds of mohair that brought thirty cents a pound.) Sixteen percent of the

Lambing season.

families accounted for fifty-six percent of the total income from wool sales.

In July all sheep and goats in the area are subjected to a prophylactic dipping under the direction of B.I.A. range authorities. Until recently, the process was handled at a single station near the chapter house. In 1970 the event was scheduled at five different windmill locations spaced across the region on five separate days during the last of the month.

In general, the summer months are times of intensive herding. and the activity places many demands on the Navajos. In the first place, if range foilage is to be properly exploited, long hours must be spent with the animals in the fields. Also, because of the limited water supply, ranchers must either haul water or drive their flocks, periodically, to one of the area windmills or ponds.

October brings lamb sales. The Navajos take their lambs and old ewes they have chosen to sell to the corral and scales behind the chapter house where the trader sets up his operation, spending the day weighing and buying the animals. Generally, the Navajos sell all of their male lambs, except for a very small percent of the wethers, and their older unproductive ewes. Only enough rams are kept in a herd to meet breeding requirements. In 1970 lambs were sold for twenty-two cents a pound, as opposed to nine and one-half cents in 1941, and ewes brought six dollars a head. Altogether, gross income for the area from 1,100 animals totaled $15,486.45. Similar to the wool sales situation, sixteen percent of the families accounted for sixty-one percent of the total animals sold.

Subsequent to the sheep and lamb sales, the Rimrock-Navajo ranchers begin to look to the advent of a new breeding season and another cycle.

The future of sheep ranching in the Rimrock area appears increasingly bleak, due to the fluctuating price of wool that fell to ten cents a pound in 1971. More and more Navajo stockmen are being encouraged to phase out their sheep and goats and begin raising cattle.

Cattle

Cattle raising as a profitable commercial enterprise is attracting a growing portion of the Rimrock Navajos. From 1951 to 1970 the number of cows grazed by local Navajos increased about 130 percent. One of the factors underlying this expansion is the fact that cattle prices have been more attractive than those brought by sheep on the livestock market. It is also generally agreed that, per sheep unit (S.U.Y.L.), raising cattle is a much less taxing industry than sheep grazing. Again, in the years since 1967 the Farmer's Home Administration (F.H.A.) has provided small-interest loans for any Navajo rancher interested in investing in cattle. By 1970 five local livestock men

Two of the many make-shift corrals in the Rimrock area.

in Rimrock were taking advantage of the F.H.A. program.

The big event for Rimrock-Navajo cattle growers occurs in the fall when they sell their cows. In 1970, cattle sales were held on October 21, the day before sheep and lamb sales. The event was staged at the chapter-house corral, and buyers from Albuquerque paid from thirty-four to thirty-six cents a pound for beef on the hoof. Total income from the transactions amounted to about $10,000.

Several factors suggest that the commercial cattle enterprise will continue to take on a greater significance for Navajo ranchers in Rimrock. A cattle association has been formed, more of the Indians are applying for the F.H.A. loans, and the awareness that cows are a much better investment than sheep is beginning to outweigh traditional commitments.

Horses

Horses have played an important role in both the entertainment and vocational aspects of the lives of the Rimrock Navajos since they first settled in the area. Because of the horse's role as a symbol of prestige, the tendency is still for the Navajo to own many more of the animals than he can use efficiently.

According to B.I.A. records, the Navajos owned about forty fewer horses in 1970 than they did in 1951. No longer were the Rimrock Navajos dependent on the horse for transportation, except in limited instances. However, many farmers used the animal for plowing and other heavy tasks, while ranchers employed it for herding sheep and roping cows. Still, the horse's primary function was one of providing pleasure and prestige for its owner.

One of the responsibilities assumed by the Navajo horse in 1970 was that of rodeo animal. The Rimrock-Navajo Rodeo, usually held in August, had become an important annual event and attracted most of the local talent that could afford the moderate entry fee. Again, many of the Navajo horsemen traveled to other parts of the state to compete in a variety of rodeos. While the Indians tended to fare rather poorly in competition with white cowboys in events such as steer- and calf-roping, due to the superiority of the Anglo-bred quarterhorse, they performed well in the riding events and occasionally brought home sizable purses.

Farming

Decline

Local Navajos have farmed since they first settled around Rimrock following the Fort Sumner experience. Despite the fact that methods have been improved over the years, with instruction from both the Zunis and the Mormons, environmental conditions have limited the profitability of the enterprise. The Rimrock area is simply not suitable for agriculture..[4]

In 1941 the Rimrock Navajos farmed approximately 3,000 acres, and by 1950 this had fallen to 1,085.[5] Twenty years later the figure had dropped even lower to 800 acres, even though there were twice as many people in the area. Similarly, while there were four families who still planted on a substantial scale in 1952, by 1970 there was only one unit that used more than twenty acres for dry-farming purposes.[6]

Besides the limitations placed on agricultural pursuits by geographical conditions, other factors have accumulated to curtail the productiveness of the Navajo's farm in Rimrock. The Navajo fields are generally ragged and irregular in their arrangement. Crops are frequently planted late in the season. Also, the Indians often use poor-quality seed, while their cultivation methods are usually unsystematic, and animal pests regularly play havoc with the growing crops. Perhaps the greatest problem affecting the recent demise of the farming vocation has been the lack of a consistent water supply. As Chavez Begay once told me:

> We used to grow a lot of corn and beans. But there was water then. Now it's too dry; too dry. You plant everything, but nothing comes up anymore. We used to have it pretty good, but we can't grow anything anymore; too dry.

The principal crops cultivated by the Rimrock Navajos in 1970 were maize, beans, squash, and melons, although several of the more prosperous ranchers grew a few acres of alfalfa for winter feed, and several households raised some garden vegetables for home use.

Agricultural Cycle

The farming year begins in April for the Rimrock Navajos. Fields are cleared and made ready for plowing in that month. In late May and early June the ground is broken and the seeds are planted. Corn is generally planted first, followed by the beans, squash, and melons.

After the young plants begin to break through the ground in

early July, hoeing activities are gradually curtailed, so that the fields receive very little attention in late July and early August. In years past there were many ceremonial procedures employed during this period to insure a good crop, but according to local informants, very few Rimrock Navajos were still observing the ritual customs by 1970. During the latter part of August some of the produce is ready for limited table use, and, although the practice is diminishing in importance, some corn pollen is still gathered during this month for ceremonial purposes.

September is harvest month. The corn is gathered first. Some is eaten during this time. The rest is either put aside for seed or steamed and dried for storage and future use. The squash and melons are collected next and then dried and stored. Later the cornstalks and the alfalfa are cut and dried to be used for livestock feed during the winter months. The beans are the last crop to be harvested. After allowing them to dry in the fields, the Navajos gather them, thresh them by hand, and store them in 100-pound sacks. With the completion of the bean harvest, the agricultural year comes to a close, for the Navajo farmers have very few, if any, crop-related activities during the winter.

In 1970, total farming income for the Navajos in the area amounted to approximately $10,000.

Wage Work

More and more Rimrock Navajos are working for wages, and the cash derived from this source is assuming a growing importance in the local economy. In the 1940s wage work was minimal. According to Landgraf a few Navajos worked for Anglo farmers or ranchers as fieldhands, a job for which they were paid $2 a day, or $1.50 a day plus meals.[7] On the other hand, by 1952 at least fifty percent of the Navajo families in the area were dependent on cash from wage work.[8] In that year the majority of the wage income was earned either on the railroad or in the sawmill. Other forms of employment in which the Navajos were engaged at that time included logging, sheep herding, farm and ranch work, odd jobs, forest-service work, and cotton picking.

Whereas in 1952 wages had accounted for about twenty percent of the total Navajo income in the area, by 1970 this had risen to almost forty percent. Railroading and working in regional sawmills were still important income sources, but were assuming a much smaller proportion of total wage opportunities. Several of the Navajos were hired locally by the trader, a construction company, and a service station. The new high school and the elementary school employed a wide range of Navajo personnel as instructional aides, bus drivers, cooks, and maintenance workers. Local missionary efforts were also dependent on several of the Indians who received regular wages for their services. By 1970, though, the largest single employer engaging local Navajo help was the federal government. Employing a total of sixty-five persons during the year at one time or another for jobs ranging from road construction to secretarial help, the government paid out almost $260,000 in wages in 1970. In total, wage work accounted for well over $500,000 of the total Rimrock-Navajo income in 1970 (*see* Table 6).

Welfare

Over the past thirty years the number of welfare recipients among the Rimrock Navajos has increased dramatically, and assistance income has become an essential element in the local economy. Welfare income was hardly a consideration in 1941. The Navajos occasionally received small relief checks, and a few others drew federal pensions, but the income from this source was proportionately insignificant.[9] By 1951, however, government assistance had taken on new dimensions, and in that year over $20.000 was paid out to local recipients through such programs as Aid to Dependent Children (A.D.C.), Old Age Assistance (O.A.A.), and Aid to the Needy Blind (A.N.B.).[10]

By 1970 money received from welfare payments comprised about thirty percent of the total cash income of the Rimrock

Navajos. In addition to the programs administered by the state —A.D.C., O.A.A., A.N.B., welfare benefits contained under the rubric "public assistance"—the B.I.A. distributed "general assistance" funds for both permanent pension and temporary hardship cases. The Rimrock Navajos qualify for the latter seasonally, depending on the financial situation of the particular family head. During the winter months, when wage-work opportunities were more limited, as many as seventy-five individuals were enrolled and received monthly general-assistance checks in amounts that ranged from ninety to 250 dollars, according to the number of dependents claimed by the recipient. The number of persons on general assistance dropped to as low as thirty during the summer months when other income sources were more plentiful. Overall, in 1970 some 130 people received a total of more than $150,000 in welfare through both public and general assistance.

Ten-Days Project

The largest single amount of cash distributed by the Navajo Tribe in the Rimrock area is the allocation for the operation of the Ten-Days Project. Under the jurisdiction of the local chapter president, $11,400 is spent annually to employ Rimrock Navajos for ten days at a time to undertake such jobs as building roads, cutting fence posts, fixing corrals, constructing hogans, or weaving. Those selected by the chapter leadership to work in 1970 earned $1.25 an hour—foremen made $1.50—and were restricted to three projects during the year. The main intent of the program is to provide income for unemployed Navajos and to handle small, local-development problems. Direct return on the investment is limited to the occasional sale of fence posts and the annual rug auction at which those items woven during the Ten-Days Project are sold to the highest bidders. In 1970 the auction was held in October and approximately fifteen rugs were sold for prices ranging from $35 to $125. The money received from the sale of items produced during the project is

Table 6

Rimrock-Navajo employment and total income in 1970

Type of job	Number employed[*]	Income
Government		
B.I.A. (Construction, dorm, clerical)	27	$186,300
Indian Health Service	2	12,000
O.N.E.O. programs	7	35,100
Tribe	1	1,100
Other	7	25,100
Subtotal	44	$259,600
Commercial, educational, tribal, and agricultural		
Local		
Trading post	2	$ 3,000
Penny Construction	4	6,000
Navajo high school	35	61,000
Elementary school	6	13,800
Texas Stopover	1	1,500
Ranch hands	10	17,000
Mission workers	4	4,000
Tribe	50	13,000
Miscellaneous	20	3,000
Nonlocal		
Railroad	10	45,000
Railroad retirement	(10)	23,000
Wingate depot	1	5,000
Sawmill	11	24,000
Subtotal	154	$219,300
Total	198	$478,900

* This figure includes part-time, full-time, and temporary employees.

retained by the local chapter and delegated to community-improvement purposes.

Miscellaneous Economic Activity

Other minor sources of income for the Rimrock Navajos include handicrafts, ceremonialist fees, trading, and the sale of firewood and fence posts. In 1951 handicrafts—rug weaving, beadwork, and silversmithing—brought in about $1,500.[11] By 1970 that figure had dropped to less than $200. Most of the rug weaving in the area was done in conjunction with the Ten-Days Project, beadwork was of minor economic importance, and there were no longer any active silversmiths in Rimrock.

The Navajo men in the area who perform traditional curing ceremonies are employed only on limited occasions and actually realize very small amounts of cash as a direct result of their services. Chavez Begay still performs Blessing Way and charges a minimum of $5 per sing, but admits that he rarely makes more, and in some instances is simply given an old sheep. In 1970 he was involved in less than ten performances, so it is unlikely that he received more than $50 in total remuneration during the year. Since he was perhaps the most active of the four or five men in the community who called themselves "medicine men," I am suggesting that less than $200 was collected locally in the form of such professional fees in 1970.

Most of the money spent by the Rimrock Navajos for hiring specialists, such as hand-tremblers and ceremonial practitioners, is invested in other parts of the state and the Reservation. The general feeling is that local performers are not as competent as those from outside the community. This attitude is reflected in the larger fees paid to specialists contracted from surrounding areas.

The frequent demand for firewood or fence posts by Rimrock Anglos provides an opportunity for Navajos to earn a few dollars. Because of the unsystematic and informal nature of this demand, estimating cash flow is difficult. However, it is known that most of the Anglos in the area rely heavily on one Navajo in particular for timber materials, and that he realized about $30 a month from such sales in 1970.

While trading is still an important economic activity among the Rimrock Navajos, whether to fulfill ceremonial obligations or to meet immediate household needs, exchange value itself is actually insignificant. In 1970 exchanges in items like lambs or hay were exercised, and, within certain limits, equivalent in value so that no one party realized any capital gains by means of this traditional process.

In summation, the total income realized by the Rimrock Navajos from these miscellaneous sources in 1970 fell approximately $1,500 short of the $4,500 that Kluckhohn recorded for 1951.[12] The reasons for the depreciation are to be found in the decline of the handicraft industry and the advent of the complementary role of the Ten-Days Project.

Total and Per Capita Income

Because of the unreliability of the B.I.A. figures, the flexibility of income estimates, the temporary nature of most Indian employment, and the changing valuation of household consumption, the calculation of total and per capita incomes for the Rimrock Navajos during any period of time is extremely difficult. However, within certain limits, the totals have a definite significance and are important for understanding economic behavior as well as planning various government and tribal programs.

According to my calculations, the per capita income of the Rimrock Navajos increased almost 500 percent in the twenty years prior to 1970. Kluckhohn arrived at a figure of $230 for 1950, as compared to my $1,046 for the later date (see

Unemployment

The complexity of the Rimrock-Navajo economic situation makes it practically impossible to calculate unemployment rates Table 7).[13]

Table 7

Rimrock-Navajo total income (1970)

Annual Indian employment and income (local)

	Man years	Full-time	Total	Income: wage	Income: property
Farming and ranching	80	34	200	$ 17,000	$35,000
Commercial	4	1	7	10,500	
Educational	22	14	41	74,800	
Mission	1	0	4	4,000	
Government	44	27	65	259,600	
Tribe	4	0	50	13,000	
Miscellaneous	1	0	20	3,000	
Subtotal	156	76	387	$381,900	$35,000
Home consumption					$18,000
Total				$434,900	

Annual Indian employment and income (nonlocal)

	Man years	Full-time	Total	Income: wage	
Railroad	8	6	10	$ 45,000	
Railroad retirement	–	–	(10)	23,000	
Sawmill	6	0	11	24,000	
Miscellaneous	1	1	1	5,000	
Total	15	7	22	$ 97,000	
TOTAL Employment Income				$531,900	

Welfare, compensation, and subsidies

Public assistance	$ 58,800
General assistance	91,700
R.E.A.P. subsidies	10,000
Total	$160,500

Table 7 (Continued)

Value of goods and services	
Commodities	$ 50,000
Medical services (P.H.S.)	110,000
Property tax exemption	5,000
Management benefits under trust	433,600*
Total	$598,600
GRAND TOTAL PERSONAL INCOME	$1,291,000
Per capita personal income (Population: 1,234):	$ 1,046

for any particular period of time. If I take the total number of man years (155) worked by the Rimrockites in 1970 and divide it by the total work force (502), I get an unemployment rate of sixty-nine percent for that year. However, this figure includes all Navajo housewives who do not work outside the home and combines temporary, part-time, and full-time employment. As such it does not project an accurate unemployment picture.

For purposes of this investigation, sample members were classed as unemployed only if they were out of work at the time I conducted the census and did not have farming or ranching responsibilities large enough to qualify as a full-time occupation. On this basis, twenty-three percent of the employable males in my sample, which represented about forty percent of the total community, were classed as unemployed in the fall of 1970. Had the survey been run during the summer months, that figure obviously would have been lower.

Perhaps the most meaningful statistic in the area of employment figures for the area is the fact that only fifteen percent of the total work force had regular full-time jobs in 1970.

* This figure includes public buildings and road construction cost, dormitory operation fees, and the cost of other government services in the area, excluding medical.

Household as Functional Economic Unit

The unit, the group, and the outfit, have generally had fairly well-defined economic functions among the Rimrock people. Sharing, cooperation, assigned responsibilities, and other characteristics of traditional Navajo economic activities have in the past attained an almost predictable regularity as a result of rules inherent in patterns of social organization.

While these laws governing social interaction still guide Navajo household activities in the Rimrock area, the situation created by the growing importance of wage incomes has brought a new irregularity to unit- and group-economic interaction.

Traditionally, the attitude that prevailed among the Navajos was one of shared ownership and responsibility, the former defined by immediate needs and the latter by sex and age. Ideally, the advent of cash incomes should not have disrupted the system, and in some cases it has not. For example, Jane Yazi was living with her father in 1970 and claimed that things still just took care of themselves:

> My father always told us that everything belonged to everyone in the family unit. If anybody needed anything they just took it. . . . Most of the time, those that work outside don't give money to the rest of the family at home, but they do buy food and sometimes clothes.

Nonetheless, in some cases, members of a household who have an outside job simply ignore any responsibilities they might have to other members of the family. In such instances a resentment develops among coresidents, and often the uncooperative individual is asked, usually by his parents, either to contribute to group finances or move to another area.

The increased mobility of the Rimrock Navajos has created another family economic problem. When children go away to live and work in another part of the state or country, they are normally expected to remember their parents and other kinfolk they have left behind. As one informant expressed: "Navajo children are taught one basic thing. When you leave home you still owe a great deal to your parents." Most of Rimrock's mobile youth remember this responsibility and regularly send money back home. Again, most parents have come to expect this gratuity, and in many cases it has become a motivation for urging children to get an education and, concomitantly, a better job. Navajo parents tend to be very open in the demands they place on their working offspring. One Navajo girl in the area employed outside the home cited a recent case in which she and her sister gave their father a new pickup truck for Christmas. His immediate response was an unabashed request that they furnish him with additional funds for insurance.

The mobility situation fosters difficulty when the traveling children forget their parents. Many of the Rimrock Navajos bemoan the fact that their son or daughter has moved to "the city" and no longer maintains contacts with home. Others complain about the irregularity or inadequacy of the funds received from working children. The rationale defining the majority of these complaints is the simple observation: "After all, we raised them. They should remember us."

Despite the problems and the antagonisms between children and parents often brought on by the wage income and migration experience, the cash flow into the community stimulated by the sense of family responsibility has had a significant effect on the local economy. Unfortunately, there is simply no way to estimate the total income derived from this source.

Credit

Since the establishment of the first trading post in Rimrock in the late 1880s, credit has been a way of life with the Navajos. Kluckhohn reported a per-person indebtedness of approximately $100 in 1951.[14]

By 1970 per-person indebtedness among the Rimrock Navajos had risen to well over $200, but not all of it was owed to the trader. Many of the Navajos had bank loans on pickup trucks and automobiles, and a few had charge accounts at

The trading post.

At the trading post.

Gallup department stores. Again, the local trader only had fifteen livestock accounts by that time, for with few exceptions most of the Rimrock Navajos had monthly incomes. Also, according to trading-post records, approximately thirty percent of Navajo buying in 1970 was on a cash basis.

Extending credit on pawned items has always been a profitable enterprise for local traders. Interest is charged on the money loaned, and, if the owner does not return to repay his debt and claim his pawn within a reasonable length of time, the trader may sell the belonging, often realizing a substantial profit.

Critics of trading activities, in particular those relating to the extension of credit and the handling of pawned property, have recently brought pressure on the New Mexico state legislature resulting in the passage of a "Pawn Industry Bill." The new law sets a maximum interest rate of four percent per month and provides that the pawned item can not be sold to pay the cost of the loan until at least three months after the loan is due.

While traders have always had methods of collecting, so that bad debts have only a small effect on profit margins, the Navajos in the Rimrock area have generally been unsuccessful as creditors. Money loaned to a friend or kinsman has in most cases eventually become a gift. Because of this, two attempts made by ambitious Navajo entrepreneurs in the forties to establish trading stores ended in financial disaster.

Although the problems that might limit a Navajo's extension of credit to kinsmen were not as evident in 1970 as they were in 1950, no new attempts had been made to institute a local, Indian-controlled business.

Consumption

Consumption patterns of the Rimrock Navajos have changed only slightly in recent decades. In 1970 they bought more fresh meat, fresh fruit and vegetables, and snack items, such as potato chips and candy, than they had twenty years before. The most notable changes, however, occurred in the cosmetic field. According to the Rimrock traders, the Navajos in 1970 purchased volumes of hair spray, mouth wash, after-shave lotion, hair cream, and under-arm deoderant. The post proprietor contended that, if patent medicines and cosmetics are considered jointly, many families spent as much as twenty-five dollars a month on drug items.

Alcohol is an important consumer good for a small portion of the Rimrock Navajos. In 1970 they invested heavily in the brewing industry, but the problem in Rimrock has never approached the proportions of that on the Reservation or in the checkerboard areas. According to the owner of the El Sombrero, the only outlet for alcoholic beverages in the immediate vicinity, there were only about twenty-five regular drinkers among the Rimrock Indians in 1970. Cheap wine was by far the largest selling item, and the heaviest drinker in the area claimed he spent about $600 that year to finance his habit.

While it would probably be safe to estimate that less than $15,000 was spent by the Rimrockites on wine, liquor, and beer in 1970, large amounts of money were lost on weekend drinking sprees to small-time conartists and thugs. Gallup, for example, is a dangerous place for a Navajo to drink, and the more experienced have learned to either avoid the risky night spots or let a sober wife carry their cash. Others simply refuse to go there to drink.

Additional expenditures of area Navajos in 1970 included money for clothes, fabrics, gas, oil, and livestock feed. Also, traditionalists spent substantial cash outlays for ceremonial activities. One older Navajo in Rimrock held a four-day Ghost Way ceremony in the fall of that year, hiring a specialist from Bluewater and inviting members of his wife's outfit. He has estimated that the total cost of the affair, including fees, food for his guests, and transportation, was approximately $100.

Economic Trends

By 1970, agricultural acreage and yield was decreasing in

Rimrock, livestock numbers were being depleted, credit was on an upswing, living conditions were gradually improving, the number of jobs and the total income from government- and tribal-sponsored activities was continuing to outdistance industry-related figures, and a move to a more unified economy was evident.

Economic development continues to be a primary problem for the Rimrock Navajos. The shrinking profitability of the agricultural enterprise, the lack of new employment possibilities, and the overall lack of productive potential in the area have been the principal impediments restricting development.

In general, it would appear that the most evident trend in the Rimrock-Navajo economic picture in 1970 was the growing dependency on state and federal welfare. Despite the incipience of a promising commercial-cattle industry, other avenues are limited, so that barring major industrial development in the area, welfare rolls will continue to expand in proportion to population growth.

TRADITIONALS, MORMONS, AND NAZARENES: COMPARATIVE ECONOMIC BEHAVIOR

The three religious groups I have isolated among the Rimrock Navajos reflect some distinctive economic tendencies. These basic differences become even more significant when the three samples are grouped in terms of churched and nonchurched Navajos, pitting the Nazarenes and the Mormons against the traditionals. The comparison from this perspective also suggests that mission participation has broad economic implications extending well beyond the triviality of free Bibles, "hallelujah's," and friendly handshakes.

In this section I am comparing the economic behavior of these groups; in most situations this means the Navajos who have been under the direct influence of one of the missions versus those who have not. The comparative analysis focuses on a wide range of economic categories including special training, income, jobs, mobility, and job performance. The controlling purpose in the comparison of these data is to isolate specific differentials defining the economic behavior of the Christian Navajos versus that of the non-Christians.

Economic Behavior

The question of the universal meaning of "economy" has long been the preeminent issue in economic anthropology. In order to focus on the main theoretical issue of the analysis —specifically, the problem of the relationship between religious change and economic behavior—I am attempting to avoid the definitional dilemma by dealing with economic categories that would generally be acceptable to economists and anthropologists alike within this context.

This investigation is predicated on a very broad, flexible, and yet fundamental understanding of economy, although it is not without its critics.[15] By economic behavior I mean that behavior having direct and primary bearing on the production, distribution, and consumption of goods and services defining man's material existence.

The Sample

As mentioned in the Introduction, the samples—Nazarene, Mormon, and traditional—actually comprehend a total of 621 Rimrock Navajos. However, in terms of actual comparisons and computations, the number of individuals involved seldom approaches that figure, due to the fact that specific criteria limit the size of the sample employed in particular problems. For example, the criterion of "economic responsibility" restricts the number of persons who can justifiably be included in the comparison of the two groups—churched and nonchurched—in such categories as employment, income, and education. On

Table 8

Formal education of the Rimrock Navajos:
by religious group and generation (1970)

	Number of individuals	Education: total number of years	Education: average number of years
Generation 1			
Traditional	29	44	1.5
Mormon	7	12	1.7
Nazarene	20	43	2.1
Total	56	99	1.8
Generation 2			
Traditional	73	388	5.3
Mormon	31	228	7.4
Nazarene	46	492	10.7
Total	150	1,108	7.4
Generation 3			
Traditional	17	120	7.1
Mormon	4	60	15.0
Nazarene	5	69	13.8
Total	26	249	9.6
Totals (all generations)			
Traditional	119	552	4.6
Mormon	42	300	7.1
Nazarene	71	604	8.5
TOTAL	232	1,456	6.6

the other hand, disability, old age, and retardation often limit the comparative utility of a particular sample member. Again, the unavailability of certain types of data in several situations precludes the possibility of using other individuals in some of the comparisons.

In general, my sample is composed of seventy-one Nazarenes, forty Mormons, and 124 traditionals that I have classified as economically responsible. Within this group, the average Nazarene is 37.9 years old, married, and has 4.1 children; the typical Mormon is 38.8 years old, married, and has 4.3 children; while the average traditional is 38.3 years old, married, and also has 4.3 children.

Education

The number of years of education that the individual Rimrock Navajo has received has a direct bearing on his English-laguage skills, and in recent years, the type of job or jobs that he has been able to obtain. Educational status is thus an important indicator of economic behavior.

Nazarenes and Mormons tend to have more formal education than do the traditionals. In fact, the churched Navajos on an average have 3.4 more years than do the nonchurched (*see* Table 8).

At the second generation level, the distinction between the two major groups in the area of formal education is even more significant. Also, when only the women in the sample are considered, the differentials are greater than those for the two groups as a whole. The average churched female among the Rimrock Navajos has 3.8 more years of formal education than does her nonchurched counterpart (*see* Table 9).

Thirty-two percent of the nonchurched sample have no formal education at all while the same statistic for the churched group is only seventeen percent. On the other hand, forty-two percent of the Christian sample, as opposed to only twelve percent of the non-Christian faction, has at least a high-school education.

Table 9

Formal education of Rimrock–Navajo women:
comparison by religious affiliation (1970)

	Number of women	Education: total number of years	Education: average number of years
Traditional	74	258	3.5
Mormon	23	139	6.0
Nazarene	40	319	8.0
Total	137	716	5.2

Special Training

Of the 210 persons in my sample who can be considered potentially employable, ten percent have some type of special training. This vocational education, usually undertaken subsequent to high-school graduation, consists of the development of one of several types of skills; instructional aide, dormitory administrator, heavy-equipment operator, plumber, or electrician. In the sample, seventeen percent of the churched but only three percent of the nonchurched have a year or more of vocational training.

Employment

The Rimrock Navajos are employed in a wide range of jobs as farmers, ranchers, secretaries, teachers, instructional aides, clerks, clergymen, construction, and railroad workers (*see* Table 6). Ninety-two members of my sample, including both male and female, had jobs in the fall of 1970. For purposes of this investigation I have divided these jobs into eight basic types (*see* Table 10).

Forty-one percent of the churched Navajos in the sample have professional and clerical positions, as opposed to only eight

Table 10

Types and numbers of jobs of Rimrock Navajos:
comparison by religious affiliation (1970)

Job type*	Traditional		Mormon		Nazarene		Total	
	Male	Female	Male	Female	Male	Female	Male	Female
1	0	1	1	2	7	2	8	5
2	2	0	2	2	3	7	5	10
3	2	0	1	0	5	0	8	0
4	6	3	4	3	6	3	16	9
5	7	0	4	0	4	0	15	0
6	4	0	2	0	2	0	8	0
7	0	0	2	0	1	0	3	0
8	4	0	1	0	0	0	5	0
Total	25	4	17	7	28	12	68	24

*Types of jobs: 1) professional, 2) clerical 3) skilled, 4)
unskilled (construction-maintenance), 5) unskilled (ranching-farming),
6) railroad, 7) sawmill 8) armed service.

percent of the nonchurched. Similarly, fifty-seven percent of
the traditionals employed have unskilled jobs, while the same
figure is only forty-eight percent for the others. Again, percentage differentials are even more significant when only second-
generation personnel in the sample are considered.

Fifty percent of the first-generation Rimrock Navajos in
1970 considered themselves to be full-time ranchers or farmers,
but only eight percent of their offspring could classify themselves
in a similar role. Again, the percentage of professional, clerical,
and skilled employees increased by thirty-one in the span between
the two age groups. This shift tended to be more pronounced
among the churched group than the nonchurched.

Unemployment

As suggested in an earlier section, it is extremely difficult to treat the local unemployment problem. In the census I conducted in the fall of 1970 the question of employment was put directly to the individual Navajos themselves. If they considered themselves to be employed, in other words had a regular job that provided a systematic income or were gainfully utilizing their time ranching or farming, I recorded the specific nature of their occupation. Chavez Begay, for example, had less than fifty sheep and farmed only about twenty acres, yet he considered himself a rancher. In most cases, on the other hand, those who were literally unemployed or not productively engaged raising livestock or crops were quite candid in admitting their jobless state.

Overall, of the 210 potentially employable Rimrock Navajos in the sample, 118 persons, or fifty-six percent were unemployed as of the fall of 1970. When only the males were considered this figure fell to twenty-three percent. However, in all fairness to the Rimrock-Navajo women, they were classified as jobless if they were not involved in any occupation beyond routine household responsibilities.

In the comparison between the two main religious classifications, the unemployment rate among traditionals outdistanced that characterizing the other group's activities in every category. Perhaps the most significant statistic here is the female-employment figure. With fewer potentially employable women in the sample, the churched group had almost four times as many working females as did the nonchurched.

Welfare

Approximately three times as many of the non-Christian population in the area received some form of federal or state assistance in 1970 as their Christian neighbors (*see* Table 11).

Job Efficiency and Performance

In contrast to the general attitude that Willems found to prevail among Brazilian businessmen regarding the advantages

Table 11

Percent of potentially employable Rimrock Navajos receiving some form of welfare (other than social security, compensation, or commodities) during the fall of 1970: compared by religious affiliation

	Nonchurched	Churched	Total
Welfare	43%	15%	29%
No Welfare	57	85	71
Total	100%	100%	100%
(Number of cases)	(107)	(103)	(210)

of hiring Protestant converts because of their loyalty and honesty, employers in the Rimrock area claim to pay little attention to the religious affiliation of job applicants or employees.[16] According to one Gallup businessman :

We never pay any attention to what religious affiliation a Navajo might have. There's not even a place for it on our application forms. There are so many kinds of religions and missions around the Reservation these days that you never know what a guy's going to tell you about the church he belongs to. It has never seemed to make that much difference.

However, when I conducted a series of interviews in the area with men who either employed or supervised local Navajos, I was able to make several observations regarding the overall job performance of the churched as opposed to the nonchurched Indians in Rimrock. On the basis of a "Supervisory Rating Form," supervisors were asked to rate their workers in ten areas on a scale from one to seven, from worst to best.[17] Of a possible fifty-five local, Navajo employment situations in the Rimrock area, I was able to get a total of thirty-six ratings, nine of which were rejected because of the inability to class the individuals in one of my three religious groups with any reliability. In most of the evaluations, the process was handled rather conservatively by the supervisors, the majority of the ratings falling within the four to six range. For this reason, one would not expect a very wide spread between the scores, regardless of how the forms were grouped. Still, in all ten of the categories, the average scores for the Christian Navajos were higher than those of the traditionals (*see* Table 12).

Table 12

Supervisory ratings of locally employed Rimrock Navajos:
comparison of average scores by religious affiliation

Categories	Traditional	Mormon	Nazarene	Total
1. Relationship with supervisor	5.6	5.8	5.9	5.8
2. Relationship with fellow workers	5.6	6.0	6.0	5.8
3. Ability to carry out instructions	4.3	5.2	5.1	4.8
4. Attendance	4.7	5.5	5.8	5.3
5. Dependability	4.4	5.3	5.4	5.0
6. Ambition	3.9	4.8	5.2	4.6
7. Adaptability to change	3.9	5.2	4.8	4.5
8. Consideration of others	4.4	5.7	5.0	4.9
9. Foresight	3.9	5.2	4.7	4.5
10. Accepting responsibility	4.1	5.2	5.0	4.7
Total	4.5	5.4	5.3	5.0
(Number of cases)	(11)	(6)	(10)	(27)

TABLE 12

The most significant differentials between the average scores of the churched group and those of the nonchurched in the supervisory ratings occurred in categories six and eight. The churched sample was evaluated as more ambitious and more considerate of the feelings of others.

Income

The calculation and presentation of incomes must be approached from several perspectives when one is dealing with a situation as complex as that of the Rimrock Navajos. For purposes of this analysis, I have chosen to deal with the problem of income from four different perspectives, in terms of (1) the employed individual, (2) the family, (3) the household, and (4) per capita income based on the household figures.

Individual Income

The range of salaries earned by the individual Rimrock Navajos who have regular forms of wage work extend from $600 to over $6,000 a year. The men who work for Anglo or Spanish-American ranchers often have a very regular type of employment, but make a limited amount of actual cash income, sometimes receiving meals and on-the-job housing as partial compensation. However, for many of the Navajos who pay no property tax and insignificant amounts for housing, such benefits are of little value. The largest incomes in the area belong to those few men who are employed on a year-round basis by the railroad.

Table 13

Average annual income of wage-working Rimrock Navajos:
compared by religious affiliation (1970)

Religion	Employed individuals	Total income	Average income
	Number	Dollars	Dollars
Traditional	13	$ 46,300	$ 3,562
Mormon	17	67,100	3,947
Nazarene	18	62,300	3,461
Total	48	$175,700	$ 3,660

When individual incomes for the three religious groups in the sample are compared, the Mormon group outranks the others, though in this category the traditionals' salaries are, on the average, larger than those of the Nazarenes (*see* Table 13). One reason for this is the fact that the nonchurched group total is skewed by the presence of two very high railroad-employee salaries. Again, the Nazarene total is reduced by the inclusion of several women's wages that, in general, tend to rank below those of the Navajo men. Overall though, the average salary of the typical Christian Rimrock Navajo is still $135 more a year than that of his traditional counterpart.

Family Income

This income total consists of the amount of cash taken in by a particular nuclear-family arrangement: man and wife or single individual. This figure includes all wages, assistance, and compensation. It is strictly cash income, however, and does not contain dollar values for home consumption, commodities, and the like. It is also notable that second- and third-generation figures are taken only from those situations where the family head is a direct descendant of a first-generation sample member.

In terms of family income, the Mormons tend to make much

Table 14

Average annual income of Rimrock-Navajo families:
compared by religious affiliation (1970)

Religion	Families	Total income	Average income
	Number	Dollars	Dollars
Traditional	28	$ 68,500	$ 2,446
Mormon	13	59,200	4,554
Nazarene	24	88,300	3,679
Total	65	$216,000	$ 3,323

more money annually than do either the Nazarenes or the traditionalists (*see* Table 14). The churched family makes $1,540 more a year than does the nonchurched.

When just the second-generation statistics are considered, the differences between the family incomes of the three religious groups become more significant, the average Christian family making $2,033 more a year than their traditional counterpart.[18]

Household Income

The household—or as it has been earlier defined, the unit— is an important economic cooperative among the Rimrock Navajos. For this reason, the total income—both cash, and livestock and crop equivalents—for the individual households is a vital category for this type of comparative study. Also, it is only on the basis of this datum that per capita income can be meaningfully calculated.

The household economic unit consists of the first-generation parent or parents, with their children, grandchildren, and any other persons living in the same immediate area and cooperating in the common livelihood process. It is not to be confused with the family group. The household income consists of the total cash taken in from wages, miscellaneous sales, welfare, and compensation. Also included in this figure is the dollar value of home consumption, both crops and livestock, calculated in terms of acreage and herd size, respectively, and current market prices. The equivalent worth of government goods and services, such as commodities and public health benefits, are not included. From this perspective in the sample, the Mormon Navajos are again seen as having the largest income, while that of the Nazarenes is the smallest (*see* Table 15).

Per Capita Income

The differentials between the household incomes of the several religious groups are better understood from the perspective of per capita incomes. The average size of the Nazarene household, because of the greater tendencies of this group

Table 15

Average annual income of Rimrock-Navajo household units:
compared by religious affiliation (1970)

Religion	Households	Total income	Average income
	Number	Dollars	Dollars
Traditional	20	$104,580	$ 5,229
Mormon	8	61,575	7,697
Nazarene	19	88,035	4,633
Total	47	$254,190	$ 5,408

toward neolocal residence patterns, is much smaller than that of either the Mormons or the traditionals. According to sample data, the typical Nazarene household consists of 5.8 members, while the Mormon and traditional units are comprised of 11.6 and 11.7 persons, respectively. For this reason, the comparative rank of per capita incomes in the sample is radically different than that reflected in the household figures. The Nazarene per capita income is almost double that of the traditionals and considerably beyond the Mormon average (*see* Table 16). Overall, the per capita personal income of the average churched Rimrock Navajo is almost $300 more than that of the typical traditional.

Mobility

Because of the environmental and developmental limitations of the Rimrock area, geographical mobility has become a very important category in the analysis of Navajo economic behavior. An ambitious Rimrockite has very few, if any, opportunities to practice a profession or develop a skill at home, and must, if he wants to succeed financially, go elsewhere to seek employment. In most cases, this means leaving the area against inner

Table 16

Average annual per capita income of the Rimrock Navajos, based on total household incomes: compared by religious affiliation (1970)

	Individuals in households	Total income	Average income
Religion	Number	Dollars	Dollars
Traditional	234	$104,508	$447
Mormon	93	61,575	662
Nazarene	110	88,035	800
Total	437	$254,190	$582*

*This figure does not include the "Value of Goods and Services" category used in an earlier calculation of area per capital income (see Table 7). Without that figure the per capita income for the Rimrock Navajos totals $561, very close to the sample average.

forces of traditional ties to kinfolk and the land. Often, young Navajos return to Rimrock with highly developed and special-ized skills, fully aware that their training is of little value in the area, but determined to live at home regardless of the economic sacrifices involved. Those who manage to survive in another area—usually a big city such as Denver, Los Angeles, Dallas, or Albuquerque—tend to make more money, are more consistent in their overall job performance, and develop more typically middle-class-white consumer habits than their friends and relatives back in Rimrock.

For purposes of comparing the mobility of the three religious groups in the sample, 235 individuals were classified according to their personal migration history. Five patterns were estab-lished and persons ranked according to the extent of their migratory behavior. The five categories of mobility are:

1. None (always living and working in Rimrock)
2. Have worked away while still living in Rimrock

3. Now working away from but still living in Rimrock
4. Had been living away from Rimrock, but now returned
5. Living outside the Rimrock area on a permanent basis having once been a local resident.

Since the five categories are structured so that each ascending classification on the scale represents a greater degree of mobility, the three sample-group ratings can be added together, on the basis of a one to five scale, and averaged; the higher the score, the greater the degree of mobility. In terms of this rationale, the Nazarenes were found to average 2.81, the Mormons 2.45, and the traditionals 1.57 (*see* Table 17). Overall, twenty-nine percent of the churched personnel had migrated away from the Rimrock area on a permanent basis, while this was true of only ten percent of the nonchurched.

When first- and second-generation sample figures are compared, a very significant change is revealed. The average mobility scores for both the Mormon and Nazarene samples are lower than those of the traditionals at the first-generation level, but the ratings for the second generation completely reverse that trend.

Consumer Behavior

The only general distinction between the consumer habits of the Christians and the non-Christians among the Rimrock Navajos is found in the slightly greater tendency for the latter to purchase more alcohol and tobacco items. According to the proprietor of El Sombrero, the mission members, especially the Nazarenes, are surprisingly consistent in their stand against liquor. The Mormon Navajos, in keeping with church standards, ideally should consume less tea and coffee, but of those in this group questioned on the subject, most admitted ignoring the proscriptive sanctions attached to these two "stimulants."

Business people in Rimrock generally contend that the Christian Navajos make better and more reliable customers. Perhaps their greatest asset, from the business community's per-

Table 17

Percentage of Rimrock Navajos classified in each of the five categories of mobility: comparison by religious affiliation (1970)

Mobility	Traditional %	Mormon %	Nazarene %	Total %
1. None	78	50	46	63
2. Worked away	8	10	6	8
3. Working away	3	10	3	5
4. Lived away	1	7	13	5
5. Living away	10	23	32	19
Total	100	100	100	100
(Number of cases)	(125)	(42)	(58)	(235)
(Average scores)	(1.57)	(2.45)	(2.81)	(2.09)

spective, is their promptness in handling credit responsibilities. As Horatio Phillips, one of the Rimrock traders, recently commented :

> When I see them Nazarenes taking those tithes up there to give to the missionary, I know those bills are going to be paid. You don't have to worry about over-extending credit to people that give their money to the church like that.

Change: 1950–1970

Many changes have taken place in the economic behavior patterns of the three Rimrock-Navajo religious groups over the past two decades. These changes have tended to expand and reinforce the distinctiveness of the Christian and non-Christian elements in the community. Differentials that were observable in 1950 were even more evident by 1970. The most obvious reason for this increasing distinctiveness is found in the churched faction's more rapid rate of change as opposed to the slower pace characterizing developments among the traditionals.

Rapoport observed for the 1950 period in Rimrock that the Nazarenes were generally of greater financial means than the other groups, both the Mormons and the traditionals.[19] Comparing individuals in terms of the relative wealth of the particular outfits to which they belonged, he found the Nazarenes to be "significantly wealthier" than non-Nazarenes. However, when these same individuals were compared on the basis of the wealth of their extended families, differences were not so obvious.

Rapoport determined the financial status of the Rimrock Navajos in 1950 in the basis of two indices: "the size of the trading account at the trading post and the number of sheep per outfit."[20] The outfits were then classed in terms of three categories: rich, medium, or poor. While, with few exceptions, the economic rank of the Rimrock outfits had remained relatively stable in the twenty years since 1950, it is significant that the indices and the methods of measuring wealth had changed. In 1970 sheep accounted for a very small percent of total income, and the importance of livestock- and wool-trading accounts had diminished, as more of the Navajos received regular wages or assistance checks and had turned to more cash buying. It would thus appear that, despite their heavy investment in sheep and other traditional concerns, it has been the wealthier outfits that have made the faster and more efficient adjustment to the new demands of a wage economy.

ECONOMIC BEHAVIOR AND RELIGIOUS CHANGE: A PRELIMINARY ANALYSIS

Overall, in 1970 the Christian groups were leading the traditionals in the trend toward economic rationalism among the Rimrock Navajos. This is demonstrated by their performance in the comparative analysis of economic behavior by categories. The churched group led significantly in:

1. average number of years of education per individual
2. special training and vocational education
3. per capita personal income
4. percentage of professional, clerical, and skilled jobs
5. percentage of group actually employed
6. job efficiency and overall performance
7. geographical mobility
8. self-sufficiency or lack of dependence on welfare.

To this point, the reality of the relationship between the religious factor and economic behavior has been demonstrated by the following observations.

In the first place, the statistical comparisons of the religious groups by economic categories reflect a definite connection between church affiliation and financial rationalism.

Also, Peacock has noted that, in light of Weber's postulation that religious influences work to "restructure the *entire* life arc, . . . one would expect to see the greatest differences between those born and raised in the Protestant-ethic group versus those born and raised in another group."[21] The significance of the Protestant ethic in this particular case notwithstanding, the intensification of differentials at second-generation levels in the comparisons suggests that this is exactly the situation among the Navajos. Exposure to the churches' programs, either directly or through the home environment, during childhood and the formative years appears to strengthen the possibility of rational economic development.

Again, Navajo women have always been more active in the Rimrock missions than the men. Therefore, if participation in the programs of the nontraditional religious organizations has had economic effects, the changes evident in the behavior of the women should be more dramatic than those exhibited by the men. This is precisely the situation reflected in the statistical data. Churched females demonstrate a significant increase in economic rationalism relative to the nonchurched to a greater degree than that observed in a similar comparison between male-sample members.[22]

Recognizing that other factors have helped to bring about economic behavioral changes among the Rimrock Navajos, my objective is not to establish religious affiliation as the principal force stimulating this process. Admittedly, educational experience, military service,[23] geographical position,[24] and travel obviously have played significant and perhaps causative roles in economic change among The People in the area.

Culture change, in any of its forms, is an extremely complex process involving many psychological and situational forces, and I am concerned with only one aspect of the phenomenon, namely, those modifications of economic patterns that can be correlated with variations in religious behavior.

Again, I am more concerned with "mutual interdependence" and those "uniform modes of relationship" persisting between two sets of data, than with "causation" in the physical science sense.[25] Therefore, if the character of that relationship between economy and ideology in the Rimrock-Navajo system can be isolated and defined, I can legitimately conclude that religious change, at least in this situation, does influence economic behavior and in a specific way. This process involves more, however, than demonstrating simple statistical correlation, which may isolate but does not define the uniform modes of relationship. In other words, it tells *that* the two groups of data are related, but it does not demonstrate *how,* neither in principle nor reality.

The entire process of establishing the fact and character of a mutual interdependence between two sets of social facts involves the analysis of both the data and their specific cultural contexts from three perspectives:

1. *Statistical* : This phase of the analytic process is primarily descriptive and demonstrates the fact of a statistical relationship between the two areas of behavior.

2. *Logical* : This perspective is theoretical and involves the analysis of the mechanics by which the internal characteristics of each of these sets of data, in this case two areas of human behavior, logically influence or are influenced by structural

modifications in the other. The specific question that one asks here is simply, from a logical perspective, what events should or should not be expected in the religious-change process marking a Rimrock-Navajo's conversion to Christianity, and why? The main purpose of the logical analysis is to clarify statistical insight.

3. *Historical*: This portion of the investigation is descriptive and focuses on specific historical events that demonstrate actual or probable relationships between the two groups of data. Its principal function is to substantiate the implications of the logical perspective. In other words, if it is theoretically possible, has it in fact occurred in this situation?

SUMMARY

The Rimrock-Navajo economy is changing rapidly, as traditional pursuits give way to a total involvement in the Western wage-market system. When the economic behavior of those Navajos participating in area Protestant missions is compared with that of those still faithful to traditional, ideological tenets, however, the former manifest a more progressive pattern of economic rationality.

On the basis of my sample-group comparisons it is reasonable to assume that the churched faction, by its willingness to accept greater economic responsibility, broader job opportunities, and the inevitability of migration, is adapting better to the demands of a wage economy than are the traditionals. Also, because of this same adaptability, it appears that it is the Christian Navajos who are making a better adjustment to the deteriorating economic potential of the Rimrock area.

NOTES

1. Kluckhohn, "The Rimrock Navajo," p. 346.
2. Landgraf, p. 24.

3. Ibid., p. 62.

4. Ibid., p. 24.

5. Kluckhohn, "The Rimrock Navajo," p. 346.

6. Rimrock Files, 15 April 1952, p. 2.

7. Landgraf, p. 71.

8. Evon Z. Vogt, "Ecology and Economy," in *People of Rimrock,* eds. E. Z. Vogt and E. M. Albert (Cambridge, Massachusetts: Harvard University Press, 1967), p. 186.

9. Landgraf, p. 73.

10. St. John, p. 16.

11. Kluckhohn, "The Rimrock Navajo," p. 348.

12. Ibid.

13. Ibid.

14. Ibid.

15. Robbins Burling, "Maximization Theories and the Study of Economic Anthropology," *American Anthropologist* 64 (1962): 805.

16. Emilio Willems, *Followers of the New Faith* (Nashville, Tennessee: Vanderbilt University Press, 1967), p. 178.

17. Blanchard, "Religious Change," p. 397.

18. Ibid., p. 269.

19. Rapoport, pp. 64–65.

20. Robert N. Rapoport 1970, personal communication.

21. James Peacock 1971, personal communication.

22. *See* Kendall A. Blanchard, "Changing Sex Roles and Protestantism among the Navajo Women in Rimrock," *Journal for the Scientific Study of Religion* 14 (1975): 43–50.

23. Adair and Vogt; Evon Z. Vogt, "Navajo Veterans," *Peabody Museum Papers* 41, no. 1 (1951).

24. Kluckhohn, "The Rimrock Navajo," p. 338.

25. Clyde Kluckhohn, *Navajo Witchcraft* (Boston: Beacon Press, 1944), pp. 56, 124.

4

Justifying the Economic Advantages
of Saintliness

Peter Antonio is Navajo. He is twenty-seven years old, born
and raised in a hogan on his mother's small allotment about
twenty-five miles southeast of the town of Rimrock itself. Peter
is a graduate of the old Rimrock High School and has had a
year's special training in heavy-equipment operation. In the past
several years he has held several different jobs—working on the
B.I.A. road crew, at the local elementary school, as an aide in
the B.I.A. Rimrock dormitory program. Throughout the several
changes, his income has steadily increased. He has a reputation
as being very bright, responsible, and of great potential. Driving
a relatively new sports car, dressing in very stylish clothes, and
apparently enjoying the pleasures of a good, regular income,
Peter appears to be adjusting well to the changing economic
scene in Rimrock. Recently, Peter married a young Navajo girl
from Crownpoint who has been teaching in Rimrock for
several years.

171

Peter's father, Willie Antonio, was from a relatively poor outfit in Rimrock, and had less than six years of formal education. In 1951 Willie had two wives and five children and was supporting his growing family with the return from a medium-sized sheep herd and two small gardens. That same year he aligned himself with the Nazarene mission in Rimrock, soon becoming one of the more active men in the organization. Under pressure from missionary Banks, Willie gave up the older of his two wives, while the younger, Alice, Peter's mother, became quite prominent in church affairs herself. Over the years the Antonios had several more children, and by the time Willie died several years ago his family was already beginning to reflect a range of economic values radically unique from those of other Navajos living in the surrounding area. One of the girls was working in Albuquerque, one was taking nurse's training in Dallas, while the others were either working at steady jobs in Rimrock, as was the case with Peter, or actively attending their respective elementary or high schools.

The situation of Peter Antonio is certainly not unusual in the Rimrock-Navajo situation and raises again, in more practical terms, the essential question I am addressing in the analysis. Given the reality of significant economic behavior differentials between the churched and the nonchurched groups in the area, what factors can be isolated that aid in the explanation of these obvious distinctions?

THEORETICAL BACKGROUND

Changing Cultural Values

Culture change is a complex process, explanations for which one must delve beyond the immediate physical realities of the contact situation. Obviously, for example, no two Navajos exposed to the same influence from the Anglo world for the same length of time will come away with identical reactions or responses. What, then, are some of the variables that account for the extensive diversification of culture-change patterns?

At its base levels, culture change is a process rooted in the minds of individual human beings.

> Institutional explanations of change, like institutional explanations of correlations, must assume a psychological foundation in the motivations of the people who initiate and support the changes.[1]

As implied in its descriptive designation, the "culture-change process" is a chronological development that moves from old patterns in the direction of a complete identification with the acculturative forces. Thus it is that value systems, with their psychological orientations, move progressively through a succession of stages toward the ideals projected by the foreign change agent. As Vogt concluded in his analysis of the effects of military life on Navajo servicemen, the culture-change process moves through an initial "imitative" stage to an eventual "internalization."[2]

Even more basic than the change process itself are the factors that initiate the acculturative developments experienced at the level of the value systems. These causes manifest themselves in the confrontation between individual needs or wants and novel possibilities.

Barnett defines the forces initiating the change process as psychological: "an individual will not accept a novelty unless in his opinion it satisfies a want better than some existing means at his disposal."[3] In general, then, I am suggesting that the culture-change process is initiated by the availability of novel options and the receptivity of individual motivations defined by needs or desires.

On the other hand, these needs are generally the products of an unsatisfactory relationship between the individual and his traditional cultural setting. Whether provoked by disruptions within the society itself or by the inability of old forms to satisfy novel individual wants, these needs are oriented in a complexity of historical events. Within this context individual patterns of nonconformity often develop; "deviance from traditional patterns of Navajo society and personal conflict and insecurity tend to lead to changes in individual value systems."[4]

Ideological value systems, or sets of beliefs, tend to be more resistant to change than those patterns underlying types of behavior other than religious. This resistance, in the process of individual religious change, creates a temporal discontinuity between behavior and the underlying belief system, the latter failing to adjust systematically and conjunctively with behavioral changes. As Kluckhohn has noted, with specific reference to the Navajo religious-change situation:

> The less tangible, more implicit aspects of Navajo philosophy have undoubtedly been altered by the impact of Christianity, ... but the underlying premises and concepts change more slowly than does behavior.[5]

Christianity has been the primary external force pressuring for change in traditional Navajo religious patterns of action and belief, and The People have generally begun to accommodate their activities to the unavoidable realities of missionary programs and influences. In this process of accommodation, though, the belief systems still resist radical modification, and those implicit ideas underlying Navajo religion persist in spite of altered modes of behavior. Nonetheless, it is obvious that certain elements of traditional religious values do begin to change in response to the external pressures of Christian ideological and nonideological programs, and synthesized belief systems are evolved representing elements of both the new and the old styles that project accommodative features. "Certainly ideas are retailored with subtle distortion of borrowed patterns of thought and behavior to swing them into line with remarkably tenacious underlying ideas."[6]

For the Navajos then, the religious-change process is a movement from general ethnohistorical events and related psychological disorientations and needs confronting novel religious opportunities and ideas to new religious behavior. From this experience, synthetic value systems accommodating traditional and modern ideological patterns are developed. Throughout this process, the implicit philosophical tendencies underlying the traditional ideology persist as the standards by which new tenets are adjusted and made intelligible.

RELIGIOUS CHANGE AMONG THE RIMROCK NAVAJOS

Rapoport in his thorough analysis of the forces underlying religious change among the Navajos in the Rimrock area, emphasized the formative role of the general historical factors, specifically, traditional cultural deficiencies coupled with the forces of social change and disorganization.[7]

In one capacity or another, the Rimrock Navajos have been undergoing the trauma of forced change since the Fort Sumner experience in the 1860s. In the area of religion they have been confronted with many external forces, the most effective being the programs of the Nazarenes and the Mormons. Specifically, the following socioeconomic factors created a historical situation that made possible changes in the religious behavior of the Rimrock people:

1. Overgrazing, mismanagement, road construction, and unfavorable weather conditions had combined to limit the productive potential of the Rimrock environment, and the Navajo had been forced to adjust to new and more diversified means of livelihood.

2. The growing importance of wage incomes and the influence of a money economy had a direct impact on traditional economic values as well as customary patterns of social organization.

3. The traditional ceremonial system of the Navajo had suffered in the past several decades due to a decline in the number of specialists and the general quality of performance.

4. In the late 1940s the Rimrock Navajos interpersonal relations were continually threatened by "intragroup hostilities and increased witchcraft."[8]

5. The increase of white goods and services created new activities and demands. From the beginning, it was clear "that the Navajo were very interested in the white man's *goods,* and not so much in his ideas."[9]

6. The increased but varied contacts with whites had a differential effect on the value systems of the Rimrock Navajos.

7. Fragmenting outfits, changing residence patterns, and other disruptive tendencies had had a "weakening" effect on Navajo social organization in the area so that relationships and kinship responsibilities were not as easily defined.

8. Changes in patterns of ownership, the prominence of the male role in the wage economy, and the decreasing opportunities for female accomplishment and recognition had very restrictive consequences for the role of the woman in Rimrock-Navajo society.

These historical factors, while having a differential impact on individual Navajos in the area, did create a general psychological receptivity to innovations.

The more immediate psychological explanations for religious change among the Rimrock-Navajo population varied with the specific situation and personal needs of the particular individual. Some of the more conspicuous pressures leading to conversion or affiliation with the Christian missions, many of which have been isolated by Rapoport and Hughes,[10] include:

1. The promise of material benefits attracted some of the Navajos. The missions, especially the Nazarene, often gave relief clothing, candy, toys, food, and other items to members of their congregations. The Christian organizations also offered service benefits, such as limited medical assistance and transportation.

2. The church program provided a common bond and a new opportunity for group interaction. Many of the Navajos, frustrated by the failings of the old system, found in the mission organization a new and meaningful social alignment.

3. The mission services offered the Rimrock Navajos, in particular the women, a new opportunity for prestige and self-expression by means of new leadership responsibility and the testimony.

4. With particular emphasis on the missions' claims to healing expertise, the Christian groups offered a new source of power to those who were beginning to question the effectiveness of traditional curing methods.

5. Christianity, seen primarily as the white man's religion, made it possible for Navajos to identify more closely with the Anglo world.

6. For some, Christianity offered a source of legitimation for newly acquired behavior in both economic and social activities.

7. Other Navajos chose to affiliate with the mission programs for a variety of practical reasons relating to immediate physical need. For example, several Navajo women had been living with their father when he died in 1970, and because his death "contaminated" their living quarters, they had no place to stay. One of the prominent Nazarene members in Rimrock, Elsie Garcia, offered them a place to stay if they would join the church. They were quite quick to oblige.

8. Because of the tendency for religious affiliation to fall along kinship lines among the Rimrock Navajos, many of the converts were drawn to the church initially by the fact that members of their group or unit had become active in church affairs.

In summarily classifying those of the Rimrock Navajos who had joined the Christian congregations, in particular the Nazarene group, Rapoport cited Barnett's thesis: "the disgruntled, maladjusted, the frustrated, and the incompetent are pre-eminently the acceptors of cultural innovation and change."[11]

THE WEBER QUESTION

The *forces* that have led individual Rimrock Navajos to

accept the novel religious practices of the Christian missions are numerous. In the same sense, the *results* have taken many forms and are evident in many areas in Navajo life in Rimrock. As the comparative economic data in the previous chapter suggests, the change in religious orientation has several possible connections with Navajo economic activities and performance. This raises the very broad question, then, concerning the nature of that relationship : specifically, in what ways did the changing religious values affect or influence economic behavior?

Historically, this particular question has been raised most adequately by Max Weber in his thesis that the birth of Protestantism influenced the development of modern, Western capitalism. As I have stated earlier, I am not attempting in this analysis to either prove or disprove Weber's theoretical propositions. I am merely taking his idea of the Protestant ethic, removing it from its historical context, and focusing it on a much more limited situation. Again, I am defining his "spirit of capitalism" in microeconomic terms, as that attitude affects individual behavior rather than broad patterns of national and international economic activity.

Weber's classic formulation concerning the historical role of Protestantism in the development of capitalism has been the subject of much negative criticism in recent years.[12] On the other hand, there are many who contend that Weber has been maligned undeservingly.[13] For the purposes of this analysis, I am satisfied with the general observation that :

> if we bear in mind that Weber regarded Protestantism as a factor which fostered the development of capitalism, and not as *the* cause thereof, we can accept his thesis as valid.[14]

Protestant Ethic

In order to analyze the nature of the relationship between the religious and economic aspects of cultural behavior within the framework initially constructed by Weber, it is mandatory that I arrive at a precise understanding of his "Protestant-ethic" concept.

The Protestant ethic as defined by Weber is a theological concept, a set of ethical precepts rooted in a world view comprehending a wrathful deity and an afterlife determined by an individual's actions in this life.

There is also a certain positive urgency to the Protestant-ethic notion. As Bendix has pointed out, because of their implicit suggestion that eschatological realities were portended in this-worldly economic performance,

> the religious doctrines of the Reformers—above all the Calvinist doctrine of predestination—introduced a basic anxiety into the believer's relation to his God, and this anxiety, so Weber's argument runs, introduced a decisive change. . . . The economic actions consistent with the "spirit of capitalism" were in significant measure efforts to relieve religious anxiety.[15]

Therefore, to the extent that the individual Protestant's behavior conformed to ethical ideals and the effects of that anxiety were mollified, the ethic performed a significant, positive function.

Overall, the Protestant ethic gave a theological depth to mundane economic pursuits. The Protestant entrepreneur felt that Providence not only tolerated his disproportionate accumulation of wealth, but, even more, used this success as a visible sign of his election as a child of God. On the other hand, the conscientious laborer received the same reinforcement by his dedication to the responsibilities of his lowly state in life.

Although I am removing Weber's idea of the Protestant ethic from its classical, historical context and raising the questions regarding the connections between religious and economic behavior in a more limited, non-Western setting, I am still depending on the original meaning and intent of the concept.

In analyzing the effect of the Christian missions on the life-styles of the Rimrock Navajos, I am specifically defining the Protestant ethic as a system of behavioral norms defining a "worldly asceticism," emphasizing the importance of work, self-discipline, and the calling, and that is directly related to underlying theological premises. Because of this necessary theological orientation, the mere presence of certain ethical proscriptions in the Christian missionary message does not mean that the Protestant ethic is automatically functional. Instead, before one can isolate a particular religious-change situation and, having noted significant differentials between the economic behavior of the traditional and nontraditional groups, conclude that the Protestant ethic is operative in that context, he must: (1) demonstrate that the ethical norms defining the behavior of the converts are consistent with those historically associated with Protestantism; and (2) show that the ideological value systems of the Christian group, either naturally or as a result of accommodative change, provide a logic for justifying their religious behavior comparable to that employed by Weber's "typical" Protestant.

Transformative Capacities Defined

As discussed in the Introduction, I am analyzing the consequences of the changing religious values of the Rimrock Navajos in terms of Eisenstadt's concept of "the internal transformative capacities of Protestantism."[16] In order to treat fully the total economic effect of the incursion of evangelical Christianity into the lives of the local Indians, I have expanded this concept to include both institutional and theological-ethical emphases. The theological-ethical capacities of Protestantism are those proscriptive norms along with the abstract ideological rationale upon which they are founded that exhibit a potential for legitimating, accelerating, and stimulating new patterns of economic behavior. It is within the theoretical confines of this category of transformative potential that Weber's concept of the Protestant ethic is operative.

On the other hand, the institutional capacities of Protestantism are the practical aspects of organizational functions that manifest similar potential for affecting economic change. These latter capacities are more direct and secular in their orientation than their theoretical counterparts.[17]

The question that concerns me now is that of the extent to which, if at all, the two groups involved—Nazarene and Mormon—reflect these basic Protestant-ethic tendencies in formal dogma and actual practice.

THE MISSION PROGRAMS: HISTORICAL, THEOLOGICAL, AND INSTITUTIONAL BACKGROUND

Historical Protestant-ethic Orientation

Nazarenes

The Church of the Nazarene, a Methodist splinter group, has a historical claim to two of the Protestant-ethic traditions outlined by Weber: classical Pietism and Methodism.[18] The connection with the former is indirect, in the sense that the Pietists were the continental forebearers of the later development of Methodism in the British Isles. Many of the theological tenets and practical programs, such as the Pietists' zeal for social work and foreign missions, filtered through the Wesley organization and were actually revitalized by the enthusiasm of the Nazarenes in the early part of the twentieth century. Unlike Calvin, the classical German Pietists—men like August Francke and Phillip Spener—with their doctrine of man as free moral agent, rejected the idea of predestination, and justified their "rational," ethical behavior on the assumption that it reinforced and expressed the closeness of their this-worldly relationship with the deity.

> In place of the systematic rational struggle to attain and retain certain knowledge of future (otherworldly) salvation comes here the need to feel reconciliation and community with God now.[19]

While the theological orientation of their capitalistic tendencies was not focused on the status of the individual in the afterlife (that is, the rationale underlying the Calvinistic ethic), the Pietists, in terms of the resultant economic behavior, effectively combined their transcendentalism with a realistic this-worldliness.

John Wesley, the founder of Methodism, adopted several fundamental themes of classical Pietism : the importance of direct communication with God, good works, and emotional assurance of moral righteousness. Under Wesley's leadership, the quest for personal holiness, or moral perfection, became the raison d'être of the new church. While the initial conversion experience was, ideally, an emotional experience, the quest for salvation eventually became an event of striving for perfection. This struggle resulted logically in a pattern of economic behavior consistent with the spirit of capitalism. Again, similar to its Pietistic ancestry, Methodism coordinated its transcendant orientation with this-worldly concerns.

In their defection from the Methodist organization, formalized in 1908, the Nazarenes affirmed their commitment to the recapturing of Wesleyan ideals, especially his conception of personal holiness.

> We believe that entire sanctification is that act of God, subsequent to regeneration, by which believers are made free from original sin, or depravity, and brought into a state of entire devotement to God, and the holy obedience of love made perfect.
> It is wrought by the baptism with the Holy Spirit, and comprehends in one experience the cleansing of the heart from sin and the abiding indwelling presence of the Holy Spirit, empowering the believer for life and service.[20]

In the attempt to manifest this holiness in their daily lives and gain the reassurance that perfection has been achieved and that the "Holy Spirit" is guiding their lives, Nazarenes take and gain the reassurance that perfection has been achieved and religious occupations. An ascetic moral code, a firm commitment to church and country, a diligence in all mundane activities, and a continuing communication with the deity, grounded in a theological anxiety and quest for perfection, make the contemporary Nazarene communicants, at least ideally, proponents of the Protestant ethic par excellence.

Mormonism

The Mormons explicitly deny any historical or theological connection with Reformation Protestantism. L.D.S. doctrines are, in many respects, radical departures from any other known forms of Christianity, but the Saints can not escape their historical orientation in Protestantism. Joseph Smith, the founding prophet of the organization and author of the *Book of Mormon,* grew up in the midst of early nineteenth-century Protestant revivalism, struggled with the competing claims of the Baptists, Methodists, and Presbyterians, and received a significant amount of religious education and training in Protestant circles. According to O'Dea, "Much can be seen in the *Book of Mormon* of the implicit mentality of the popular Protestantism of the time."[21]

The doctrines of the Saints reflect a clear Protestant-ethic orientation. Similar to Weber's ideal, the Mormons combine eschatological concerns with this-worldly pursuits. Life after death is viewed as a continuation of earthly existence, and a man's status in this world is indicative of the magnitude of his reward and position in the next. Therefore, it is imperative that he observe the tenets of a strong moral code and use his allotted time on earth wisely.

Mormons place a high premium on economic achievement. This emphasis is reflected in the financial genius of many of their contemporary leaders, the reputation of Mormons as very strongly business oriented, and the overall wealth of the L.D.S. organization.

Also inherent in the theological system of the Latter Day Saints is a strong commitment to the "American ideal." An explicit admonition that its members obey the law of the land, a pervasive frontier spirit, and a strong sense of independence and personal freedom are prominent Mormon themes.

Despite the fact that the Latter Day Saints organization can not technically be classified as a Protestant denomination, it is obvious that the Mormon ethic functions in precisely the same manner as its more orthodox counterpart.

On the basis of such orientations, it appears that both the Mormons and the Nazarenes are ideally suited for the task of implanting Protestant-ethic ideals and motivations into the religious lives of the Navajos choosing to affiliate with their mission programs in Rimrock. However, whether the transference and implantation is actually the case is another problem.

Missionaries as Directed Change Agents

From the inception of their missionary program among the Rimrock Navajos in 1946, the Nazarenes have made a concerted effort to change a wide range of Navajo customary practices, both religious and secular. The tendency was for the missionaries to identify all traditional elements from medicinal herbs to ceremonies as "the devil's business." According to Hughes, the first Nazarene missionary, Fry, "was anti-Navajo customs, antianthropologist, antibigamy, antipeyote, antisin in general."[22] In connection with the emphasis on change, the tendency was for the new organization to stress an exclusiveness and a radical either-or commitment.

In most cases, the Navajo converts have taken the message of dramatic change seriously, especially where traditional religious practices are concerned, and have made at least some token adjustments following their new religious experience. For example, Myrtle Apachio reports:

> In the old days . . . when you ate meat, there were certain parts of the sheep you weren't supposed to eat. The medicine man told you what parts to eat. . . . After I joined the church [Nazarene], I ate every bit of what he [the medicine man] told

me not to eat, and I did *everything* the opposite of what they used to say : "Don't do this and don't do that."

On the other hand, the Mormon missionaries have never made an issue of the culture-change problem. As mentioned earlier, the Saints' concept of faith and their historical understanding of Lamanite traditions have made them much more tolerant toward Navajo ways in general than the Nazarenes.

Kluckhohn has noted that, "The Mormons have been the primary agents of acculturation for more than 70 years . . . ," from the persceptive of the Rimrock Navajos.[23] However, their missionary efforts have very rarely, if ever, stressed the importance of the Navajos' making any dramatic changes in their traditional patterns of behavior, religious or otherwise. As a result, most of the Navajos who have been baptized by the L.D.S. elders make a clear distinction between the demands of the Nazarenes and those of the Mormons, and at the same time reaffirm their commitment to the old way (*'aał'kidáá'yaa k'ehgo*).

Nazarene and Mormon Doctrines: Elements Favorable to Success among the Navajos

Theologically, Christianity is a radical departure from anything Navajo. However, there are certain elements that either directly or indirectly have some congruence with basic ideas in Navajo ideology.

The areas of possible harmony between Nazarenism and Navajo religion are limited. Some converts sufficiently familiar with Navajo mythology have attempted to relate supernatural figures from the two traditions. Changing Woman has been identified with God, and Monster Slayer, the son of Changing Woman, with Jesus. "Like Jesus, he came onto the earth to 'save' the people by ridding the earth of the dangerous monsters that occupied it before mankind's emergence."[24]

An important feature of the Nazarene message is the stress on the imminence of the end of the world. While the idea is not prominent in Navajo thought, physical and social disruptions can make the idea more tenable to the suffering individual.

A theme common to both Nazarene and Mormon doctrine is the emphasis on "faith" or "divine" healings. The Navajos, with their ever-present concern with health and physical well-being, are naturally receptive to this element in Christian doctrine.

Looking specifically at Mormon theology, several basic ideas are very compatible with traditional Navajo thought. In contrast to other Christian denominations, the Saints have no conception of original sin. This unique theological position is relatively consistent with the Navajo notion that human nature is neither good nor bad. All persons contain a mixture of both qualities from birth.

For the Navajos, one of the primary means of achieving power is the attainment of knowledge. "To live successfully, one must think well."[25] Similarly, the Mormons view knowledge as a prerequisite for salvation.

Another important emphasis in Mormon thought and practice is the significance of the role of the family institution. This finds a harmonious response in the strong kinship orientation of the Navajos.

Problem of Theological-ethical Capacities: Mormonism and Nazarenism

Despite the natural congruence of several elements of Nazarene and Mormon theology with the ideology of The People, there are many negative factors that have restricted the effectiveness of Protestantism's theological-ethical capacities among the Rimrock Navajos. These disadvantages, which clearly outweigh the advantages, have been the products of, first, the natural resistance of traditional value systems toward Protestant ideology and the related inability of the Navajos to conceptualize fundamental Christian categories, and second, the failures and problems of the Mormon and Nazarene missions themselves.

BACKGROUND:
NAVAJO THOUGHT PATTERNS

While Navajo thought has no explicit philosophical principles concerning the nature or reality of the ultimate foundations of ethical behavior, there is a unifying ideological value system deeply rooted in the way of life of every individual. Most of the Rimrock Navajos are adverse to talking about abstract ideas and meanings. Explanations for religious behavior are generally rendered directly, pragmatically, and in terms of immediate, existential concerns.

For this reason, anthropologists have chosen to think in terms of implicit philosophical premises that underlie Navajo thought and behavior. These subconscious elements of traditional value systems comprehend a very logical world view. Kluckhohn has isolated and outlined these premises:

1. The universe is orderly: all events are caused and inter-related
    a. Knowledge is power
    b. The basic quest is for harmony
    c. Harmony can be restored by orderly procedures
    d. One price of disorder, in human terms, is illness
2. The universe tends to be personalized
    a. Causation is identifiable in personalized terms
3. The universe is full of dangers
4. Evil and good are complementary, and both are ever present
5. Experience is conceived as a continuum differentiated only by sense data
6. Morality is conceived in traditionalistic and situational terms of abstract absolutes
7. Human relations are premised upon familistic individualism
8. Events, not actors or qualities, are primary.[26]

The Navajo and Christianity

The implicit premises of traditional Navajo thought present

a natural ideological resistance to Christian theology, As a result, the question is often raised as to whether or not any Navajo truly understands Christianity.

Christian denominations of all types have literally inundated the Navajo with missionary programs and proselyting attempts, in both reservation and off-reservation areas, actually to the point of absurdity. For example, Deloria claims that in 1965 there were twenty-six different missions in the Farmington, New Mexico, area, serving a total of 250 Navajos.[27] Despite the volume of exposure, missionizing programs among the Navajos have generally failed, if success here is measured in terms of significant theological impact.

The theoretical failures of the Christian message in many cases have cultural explanations. Perhaps the most evident barrier to Christian doctrine presented by the Navajo situation is the language problem. In many cases, the direct translation of key concepts is impossible. In the first place, there is no word in Navajo for the general phenomenon "religion." At times the idea is translated with a phrase that refers to the performance of the ceremonial practitioner. Again, for many decades after Anglo missionaries first began to work in Navajo country, a word that described the Catholic priest and his long robe was employed in this situation. More recently the tendency has been, especially among Protestants who feel a definite historical distinctiveness from Catholicism, to speak of believing in a religion," as "stepping into a church." For example, the sentence, "John Yazzie believes in the Christian religion," is translated by Navajo interpreters as, *"Ei nee'shozhíí John Yazzie 'iidi'yáá"*; literally, this is, "John Yazzie stepped into the Christian church."[28]

The language problem is also at the heart of the conflict between the mythologies of Christianity and traditional Navajo religious categories. Although in the past, attempts have been made to translate the idea of "God," for example, either as a "holy person" (*diné diyinééh*) or as, "Holy one that is high,"[29] more recently the churched Navajos in the Rimrock area have begun to use the English word *God* directly. Thus, the Navajo speaker will refer to the Bible as *God bizaad,* "God's word." The older expression for Bible is "*Naaltsoos diyinééh*" or "holy paper."

In Navajo mythology there is no supernatural being comparable to the masculine omnipotent God of the Judeo-Christian deities, the Navajo holy people (*diné dighinii*) are not hierarchically arranged nor do they behave in any way qualitatively different from man. The concept of a transcendant deity, ultimately sacred and radically removed from the earthbound categories of human existence (for example, Barth's "wholly other" concept of God)[30] is completely foreign to Navajo ideology.

Other elements of Christian myth that do not encounter a natural receptivity in traditional Navajo thought patterns are the creation and the resurrection. In opposition to the Judaic notion that the universe is the product of a single, historical act, the Navajos conceive of the creation event as an ongoing process. On the other hand, the idea of the resurrection of Jesus is logically incomprehensible to the Navajo mind.

> Whatever the denomination bent on conversion, the Resurrection would surely be agreed on as a fundamental dogma. What does it involve? A belief in individual immortality, in sin that must be atoned for; that one individual, god-man, could endure the punishment for all mankind; a conviction that a man, having died, may live again and appear to his survivors. The last, the greatest achievement of Christianity, is positively abhorrent to Navajo psychology.[31]

The rationale underlying Western ethical proscriptions also presents problems for the Navajo conversion candidate. In contrast to the *ex cathedra* premises upon which Christian behavioral norms are structured, Navajo moral choices are based ultimately on reason and practical discourse. As Ladd has concluded, the Navajo moralist is "a rationalist par excellence."[32]

Again, unlike Christian ethical demands, the Navajo moral

code is nonauthoritarian. It is not "based on the commands of the Holy People," nor does it " cite the 'old ways' as grounds for performing the acts prescribed."[33] For this reason, the Christian concept of *sin* is difficult for the Navajo to comprehend. The commission of a wrong act is simply the result of a person's not knowing what he is doing.

Essential to the Christian understanding of sin is the idea of "guilt." While Navajo informants have been able to handle the predicate structure of the concept—for example, *yi'kedi'daalii* ("They are guilty")—they have been unable to give me a substantive form for the English notion of "guilt" as a specific entity. Guilt is obviously a reality in the traditional Navajo personality, but it is understood quite differently than the white-Christian concept.

Illustrating the inherent inability to conceptualize the sin category, Bertha Yazi once told me about a confession and confirmation experience she had while at boarding school in Fort Wingate as a fifth grader.

> I went to the Catholic church. In fact, I went there for half a year, and they started teaching us the catechism. Anyhow, there was a time when we were all supposed to have our first holy communion. We were all supposed to dress in white and everything else and we were supposed to go to the altar there and receive this bread from the priest and all that stuff. They told us on the Saturday before that we were only supposed to have water. Sunday we were supposed to go to church and have our first holy communion. . . . Saturday, too, they said we were supposed to make a confession. You go into this little room and you tell the priest all your little troubles, I guess, or things that you've done that you know is wrong and all that stuff.
>
> Well, I went there and I didn't know what kind of story to tell. I just didn't know who in the world I'd done wrong to. I just told him, "I don't have anything."
>
> He said, "Well, why did you come in here if you don't think you have anything?"
>
> So, I just got up and walked out. He came after me. I heard the door after awhile, and I looked back, and he was coming. He said, "I'm sure you can think of something. I'll give you another chance."

So I asked this other girl, "What did you say?"

She said, "You know, I made up a story. I told him my best girl friend was mad at me, and I called her all kinds of names."

So I told him the same story. Oh, I just felt real bad about it because I told him a story.

In considering the translatability of Christian eschatology into Navajo categories, Reichard concludes that: "Navajo and Christian tenets on the afterlife are antithetical."[34] In the first place, the Navajos place primary importance on the meaning of *this* life as opposed to any hypothetical postdeath paradise.

It has been reported that traditionally the Navajos have an idea of an afterworld located far to the north where the inhabitants live as they did on earth, and life is generally "better" than in this existence.[35] However, it is probably the case that the notion has been significantly influenced by elements of Christian mythology.

Whether or not the afterlife is viewed as a "better" existence, the Navajos are not motivated to proper behavior by the consideration of a possible fate in a future world.

Related to certain eschatological themes in Christianity is an evident preoccupation with death. The spirits that return from the grave to admonish the living in both the Old and New Testaments, the Crucifixion and the burial, and the idea of the Holy Spirit or Holy Ghost illustrate this tendency.

While the Navajos do not fear death as a personal experience to any unusual extent, they do exhibit an intensive phobia, typical of Athabascan peoples in general, regarding the dead themselves and their ghosts (*ch'iidii*). According to Reichard, this fear "amounts to a tribal phobia."[36] It is strange, then, that Navajos can embrace, even superficially, an ideology whose central personage is a god-man who has risen from the dead and whose personal guide to proper behavior is an "indwelling Holy Ghost."

A fundamental operation within the institutional life of the Christian church is the collection of tithes and offerings. While the notion of indirect return in the form of "heaven-sent bless-ings" is often invoked to stimulate contributions, the idea of sacrificial giving remains the primary rationale behind the financial support of church programs. Such economic altruism is incomprehensible to the Navajo, for the thought of giving with-out expectation of return is absurd.

These are just a few of the many cultural barriers that limit the effectiveness of the theological-ethical capacities of evangel-istic Christianity among the Navajos. This general analysis sug-gests that in order to explain the fact that so many Navajos have been "converted" as a direct result of Christian-missionary efforts, one must posit some form of radical ideological change. However, in line with my initial hypothesis, I am arguing that traditional belief systems are not being altered as dramatically as behavior patterns might suggest. Rather, the converts, more directly effected by institutional rather than theological-ethical capacities of proselyting groups, are developing accommodative ideological value system that synthesize the implicit philosophical premises of traditional Navajo thought with the more convenient and acceptable elements of Christian theology.

Specific Problem of Conceptualization

From my first conversations with Nazarene Navajos in Rim-rock, I sensed a definite weakness in their theological compre-hension. Even among those who had been faithful to the cause for over twenty years, like Charles Yazi and Alice Antonio, the understanding of basic doctrine was at times completely foreign to what appeared to be intended in the missionaries' messages. Even the native preachers, like Clarence Alonzo, for example, seemed to have reinterpreted, in some basic Navajo direction, many standard biblical and doctrinal statements, at least in the sense in which these were expressed in Anglo-American Nazarenism.

For purposes of testing these observations, I devised a "Religious Preference and Comprehension" questionnaire.[37] This form was administered to thirty of the longtime, Nazarene-Navajo converts, five Anglo Mormons, five past and present Nazarene missionaries in Rimrock, and eighteen randomly selected members of a large Nazarene church in Dallas considered to be representative of average, middle-class, Anglo-American Nazarenes.

The purpose of this specialized investigation, the questionnaire, the intensive observation, and the many formal and informal conversations was fourfold : (1) to compare the theological and historical understandings of Navajo Nazarenes with those of a representative Anglo congregation; (2) to statistically isolate the ideological themes stressed by the Navajo converts; (3) to analyze the extent to which, if any, Navajo Nazarenes were comprehending and internalizing essential theological concepts; and (4) to give a theoretical cohesiveness or general structure to the ideological synthesis that, as I have suggested previously, replaces individual, traditional belief systems in the process of religious change.

This particular phase of the analysis is predicated on the assumption that Protestant-ethic behavioral tendencies are related directly to specific, abstract theological understandings, and in order for the Protestant ethic to be effective in its impact on economic behavior, these theological tenets must be internalized.

Weber was quite clear in his insistence that the dictates of the Protestant ethic were rooted squarely in abstract, doctrinal understandings :

> Now these sanctions were to a large extent derived from the peculiarities of the religious ideas behind them. The men of that day were occupied with abstract dogmas to an extent which itself can only be understood when we perceive the connection of these dogmas with practical religious interests.[38]

The imperative implicit in Weber's treatise—that the effectiveness of the ethic depends on the extent to which the theological orientation is internalized—is made explicit by Bendix :

the religious beliefs of the Puritans contained incentives encouraging a personal conduct of 'innerworldly asceticism' to the extent that these beliefs were internalized—clearly a conditional assertion.[39]

Theological Problem

One of the primary concerns of the typical member of the Nazarene church is the conversion experience itself. Doctrinally, this event is referred to as *justification,* but where theological sophistication is less important it is called *getting saved.*

> We believe that justification is the gracious and judicial act of God by which He grants full pardon of all guilt and complete release from the penalty of sins committed, and acceptance as righteous, to all who believe on Jesus Christ and receive Him as Lord and Savior.[40]

The Rimrock-Navajo converts' understanding of this basic soteriological theme is limited by both language and traditional thought patterns. The Navajos use the root verb *save* to express the idea, a word that traditionally is employed to describe a type of generalized assistance. For example, the testimonial, "I got saved," is translated, *"Yiis'dáá' shit'oltíí,"* or, "I was helped." The general concept of "salvation" becomes, *"Yiis'dáána 'ill'déé,"* or, "Help comes to you."

Unlike their Anglo counterparts, the Navajo Nazarenes view the initial conversion experiences as an event of change or healing, rather than as a "forgiveness of sins." In the comparative questionnaire, 100 percent of the Dallas group defined "being saved" by selecting the answer "our sins are forgiven," while the majority of the Navajo respondents chose the phrase "we change our ways." This same tendency was evident in the results of several other questions related to the "salvation experience." Typical of this prevailing conception is Charles Yazi's response:

> I used to try and be a medicine man, way back in my early life. I used to try to be a medicine man and study all kinds

of songs and weeds for medicine, all kinds of roots. I used to study that. Finally Jesus find me and turn me around and told me to get rid of the past. I have struggled ever since. When I become a Christian I know what in my heart God tells me. Everything I had, everything I was going to be, a medicine man with it; "Throw everything off, with all your house, everything out of your house. And throw everything out of your heart for Jesus to live in." That's what God says. I throw everything out. Some say burn it. I didn't burn it; I just throw it out on the trash pile, and every songs in my mind and all the pray what I learned. I never did use it after when I pick up the Bible. I used to go to that little hot room. I used to go and get sweat, and sing inside and pray inside. I threw off all that. I didn't go no more. That's what God says.

The principal significance of the "salvation" event for the Navajo Nazarenes in Rimrock is its curing potential. Of those questioned about their conversion, approximately ninety-five percent connected the occasion with a specific injury or illness and its "supernatural" cure. Myrtle Garcia's explanation is a typical Navajo response to the question, "Why did you join the church?"

Before five years ago I used to come to church, but I still drank a lot and did other things. The doctors told me that if I didn't stop drinking I was just going to fall over; something was going to happen to me. So I quit. But after I quit there was another period there when I wasn't really strong in the church, but I found out I had something wrong with my body. I knew it was coming on. I felt it. I didn't know, but I just kind of played around with the church. I didn't really give myself. I guess the Christian people found out that I had quit drinking but they knew I was sick. So the Christian people came and told me that my body could be healed if I really meant business. Leo came and told me and that's when I really felt I should go to the Lord to heal me. . . . I did and I've been well ever since. The reason I went was because I wanted to get well. I was sick. I went to a lot of different medicine men, but they didn't help a bit. I continued to get worse, so I finally decided I was going with the church.

"Sanctification" is the idea that gives the Church of the Nazarene its theological distinctiveness, but the Rimrock-Navajo converts, despite the fact that many of them claim to have had the experience, do not appear to have grasped the ultimate significance attached to the concept. On the questionnaire, the large majority of the Rimrock group, deviating from the clear norm established by the Dallas congregation, saw those who had been "sanctified" as simply "better off than those who are just 'saved.' " The word used for the experience in translation refers to the possession of "holy air." For example, the sentence, "I got sanctified," is rendered, *"Ni'chee düya'innii shi'ilyáá,"* which literally means, "Someone gave me some holy air."

Baptism, while not as important in Nazarene circles as it is in the Mormon organization, is considered by the theologically orthodox to be simply a sacramental act by which one witnesses to his conversion and religious commitment. This concept translates very poorly into Navajo. In order to render the expression, "I was baptized," one says, *"Tsi'tsii'táá tó illyaa"*; literally, "Water was put on my head to stay." The Navajos see the primary importance of the act of baptism as affording additional protection against illness, a notion supposedly directly reinforced by Mormon-missionary efforts in the area. Elsie Pino has observed :

> People who've been baptized won't get sick as much. That's what I've heard. I think it's true. My grandma's like that. She's been a Christian for a long time and she doesn't get sick or anything like that.

In line with the traditional Navajo style of ethical reasoning, the converts in the Rimrock area interpret the "moral standards" of the Nazarene church as based on practical rather than theoretical reasons. While the typical Dallas Nazarene suggests that one should not drink, for example, because the Lord or the Bible "demands that we live clean lives," the Navajo would point to a more directly physical explanation : "we might get hurt."

Clarence Alonzo has argued:

> You should not go to the squaw dance, the *Yeibichai,* the rodeo,
> maybe the state fair, and you should not go to the medicine
> man or worship or let him worship on you with all the paints.
> You have to get rid of this old religion. If you go to the rodeo
> you might get thrown off the horse or the bull and break a leg
> or something, or you might get drunk. That's the main thing.
> If you go to the state fair a vehicle might run over you and
> you might have some kind of accident.

While it is obvious that the Navajo Nazarenes in Rimrock
have a significantly different concept of sin than do their white
counterparts in Dallas, it is not clear exactly what they intend
in their discussion of the idea. The expression, *"Baahági 'asdzaa"*
("I made a mistake"—with ethical connotations), is used to
translate, "I sin," but it appears that the same emphases coloring
their conception of "salvation" are operative here, namely,
change and healing. Logically, a person is sinning if he participates in any of the events characterizing the "old way," and
illness is the immediate sign of the results of that wrong act. On
the other hand, there is a tendency for the Rimrock Navajos to
put an unusual amount of stress on the evil of swearing. Many
of them see this as "the worst sin" and underscore the importance of the spoken word. Charles Yazi views the tongue as the
veritable focus of proper religious behavior.

> Being safe means just pray to God. Pray to God and never
> backslide and just go on to be safe; not to use any other kind
> of language, bad language, bad speech. Whenever a person's
> saved, he should take care of his tongue; not to say bad words.
> I think that's the only meaning of safe. If I get saved, if I'm
> converted, I never use any kind of bad words.

Rimrock-Navajo Nazarenes also tend to view the church
from a different perspective than do members of the Dallas
organization. The latter see the institution's primary function as
one of providing a context within which one "can seek and find
the Lord." The Navajos see the church's most important con-

tribution in its more immediately evident provisions for fun and fellowship. In opposition to Reichard's observation that, "The Navajo of my acquaintance know few Christians who enjoy their religion . . . ,"[41] the Rimrock Navajos emphasize the importance of church activities as pleasurable experiences. For this reason their favorite part of the mission program is the "on-the-grounds" dinner, which creates ample opportunity for free interaction. The revival service, with its high level of emotionalism, is also popular.

Problem of Historical and Theological Knowledge

As is to be expected, the Nazarenes among the Rimrock Navajos are much less accomplished intellectually than the Dallas group on factual matters pertaining to the Bible, church history, and theological insight. In short, the Navajos have not been exposed to the same quantity or quality of religious education, and are thus relatively unaware of great volumes of data that in reality play a vital role in the definition of the religious value systems of the typical Anglo Nazarene. For example, all of the Rimrock Nazarenes who were questioned claimed they had never heard of John Wesley. None of this same group was familiar with the Athanasian doctrinal position, so central in Christian theology, that Jesus is to be viewed as both god and man; both divine and human. Again, the recent entrance of the Pentecostal group into the area has exposed this same lack of historical and theological education. Most of the Nazarenes in the area find it difficult to isolate any significant differences between the doctrines of their church and those of the Pentecostals, two groups that in many respects represent radically distinctive ideologies.

Problem of Leadership

Cultural explanations are at the base of the greatest percentage of the conceptualization and internalization limitations characterizing the theological experience of the Navajo Christians. [The language problem and the influence of traditional thought patterns severely restrict thoroughgoing ideological change.]

On the other hand, the specific programs of the Christian missionaries who have worked with the Navajos in the Rimrock area must also share a portion of the responsibility. In the first place, the Mormons have never attempted to define the "issues" for the Navajos, nor have they ever insisted that the Lamanites deal with basic theological questions or make ideological commitments. The situation that Kluckhohn observed in 1950 with reference to the Mormon influence on the Rimrock Navajos still prevailed twenty years later : "Purely religious teachings do not appear to have gone very deep."[42]

Though the Nazarene missionaries have focused their efforts more directly on ideological change, it is obvious that they have been relatively ineffective, and in many cases their failures have been due to the ineptitude of their own programs. For example, there has been a tendency for Nazarene missionaries working in Rimrock to simply overlook formal historical and theological training on the assumption that "the Gospel story is sufficient to its own ends." In addition to this strange sense of history, the missionaries generally possess only a very inadequate understanding of Navajo language and culture. This is reflected in the translation of their messages and lessons, and the most evident result is confusion. The Navajo converts themselves often complain about this ineffectiveness in their white leadership and the limits it places on theological competence. Charles Yazi once noted :

> These Indians, they say they believe in God, but they just say it with their lips, not in their heart. They preach, but they mix up God's law and Indian law. They just mix it up. . . . The missionaries get it confused in their preaching. People don't know which way to take it. . . . My people don't understand sometimes what sin is. It's pretty hard for the missionary to explain. They don't know the language.

General Lack of Internalization

The language problem, the resistance of traditional value systems, and the ineffectivenes of the missionaries and their programs have thus combined to inhibit any meaningful internalization of basic Christian concepts by the Nazarene converts among the Rimrock Navajos. Despite the fact that religion-questionnaire results revealed no meaningful variation between the comprehensions and preferences of the Nazarene missionaries and those of the typical Nazarene congregation, these ideological values have clearly *not* replaced traditional thought patterns among the Navajo membership.

The Synthesis

While it is evident that the basic theological premises of Nazarenism are not being internalized, it is certain that some type of value change is taking place. This change, however, is not a replacement of traditional values. The persistence of Navajo value themes is evident in the theological observations of the converts themselves.

In her analysis of Navajo mythology, Spencer isolated four significant and reoccurring value themes: "the maintenance of health; the acquisition of supernatural power; the maintenance of harmony in family relationships; and the process of the young man's attainment of adult status."[43]

These same value themes lie at the base of the accommodating systems synthesized by the Navajo converts to Christianity. Health is expressed both directly and indirectly as the primary concern. The power represented in the concept of God is also an important value. This is illustrated in the heavy emphasis the Navajos place on the act of prayer. Family concerns color basic religious ideas, and ethical decisions are products of rational, practical considerations rather than of divine fiat.

In general, Navajo Nazarenism employs the biblical and

doctrinal language of its Anglo counterpart, but the ideological value systems underlying the religious experiences of the individual Rimrock-Navajo converts are more Navajo in orientation than they are Christian. "Salvation" is the realization of physical health achieved and maintained by the proper observation of the prayer ritual by means of which one participates in the assumed superior power of the Christian deity. The additional religious experiences (for example, sanctification and baptism) reinforce the initial state of well-being, as do also the explicit moral restricitions of the church's program (for example, no drinking, smoking, or dancing).

In analyzing the theoretical implications of the confrontation between traditional Navajo ideology and Christian theology, Hughes observes that:

> one is surprised at how easy it has been for some of the Navajo to adjust their thinking to concepts of an alien religion. It is all the more remarkable in this case because of the specific and antipodal nature of Navajo religion as compared to traditional Christian beliefs. . . .[44]

However, when one recognizes that the change process here is only superficially adjustive in the sense that the Navajos retain the vital ideological elements of traditional value systems, the event does not appear as "surprising" or "remarkable."

Second Generation: Problem of Theological Education

As the statistical comparisons in the previous chapter revealed, second-generation Navajo Christians, those who have grown up under the influence of converted parents, reflect more traits of economic rationalism than do their nonchurched counterparts. Differentials at this level are much more significant than those resulting from the comparison of first-generation sample members. This suggests that the churches have had a greater impact on the economic behavior of the children of original converts than on that of the converts themselves, their

doctrines or programs having been more effective at later generation levels. If this is the case, how are the children of Rimrock-
Navajo Christians influenced by the transformative capacities, in
particular the theological-ethical aspects, of Protestantism?

Traditionally, Navajo children received their religious
education from their mother's brother or grandfather (mother's
father). Sitting around the fire or in the hogan late in the evening, the young were exposed to myths about the First People
and Changing Woman, legends about the Navajo past, stories
about the origin and meaning of natural phenomena, and guides
to ethical living. The whole family often participated in sings
and other ritual activities, and young men aspiring to a career
as a ceremonial specialist turned to an appropriately trained
uncle for instruction. In general, religious training was a normal
part of the everyday routine, and by the time a Navajo youth
had reached maturity, his world had been more or less structured by meaningful ideological experience. Though ceremonial
life in Rimrock has deteriorated to a certain extent in recent
years, this is still the general pattern observed by the typical
traditional family.

On the other hand, when a Navajo family joins a Christian
church and rejects the "old way," responsibilities shift. Among
Rimrock Nazarenes, the mother has become the principal source
of the children's religious education and the authority on all
matters pertaining to Christianity. For example, when I administered the religious questionnaires to Nazarene converts in the
area, in the several situations where Navajo couples were questioned collectively, the wife was the spokesman, and while she
might challenge her husband's choice of answers, he would not
contradict and tended to follow her lead in selecting responses.

Unlike the traditional pattern of religious instruction that
has a certain degree of regularity, the Christian home program
is very unsystematic, and theological training is generally infre-
quent and sporadic. Most Nazarene mothers among the Rimrock
Navajos feel that their primary responsibility is simply encouraging the children to attend weekly church services. However, in

accordance with traditional child-rearing practices, demands are usually very flexible, and results are slight.

Despite the fact that many of the churched youth in the area are exposed to Christian programs (that is, Mormon seminary and Nazarene youth training), theological learning in this context does not go far to supplement the limited effectiveness of the home influence.

In general, the average Navajo child in a Nazarene home receives very little religious education, traditional or otherwise. As a result, the Nazarene-Navajo young person has a functional knowledge of neither Navajo nor Christian ideology, and only develops a competence comparable to that of his parents as he gets more directly and emotionally involved in the mission program.

Mormon Navajo children, while most have an even weaker theological background than the Nazarenes, do receive religious instruction in the "old way," for the Saints do not demand a rejection of customary values. For this reason, Mormon Navajos tend to have as refined an understanding of the ways of The People as do the traditionals.

In general, Christian religious education does not play a very formative role in the early lives of second-generation Mormons and Nazarenes. Even though both groups obviously receive some theological influences by way of the home, the missions, and the youth programs, the theological capacities of Protestantism are limited in their effectiveness by the same lack of internalization characterizing conceptualizations at first-generation levels.

Still, statistics demonstrate the reality of the greater modernity of the Christian Navajos' economic behavior as opposed to that of the traditionals. What forces in Protestantism have been effective at this point? If theological-ethical capacities were operative in this context, one would expect the traits of economic rationalism to be more evident among the second-generation Nazarenes than among their Mormon contemporaries. The former, as children, have been generally more exposed to Christian theology and anti-Navajo themes. Nonetheless, despite the stronger traditional orientation of the Navajo Saints, in the comparison by economic categories between second-generation Mormons and their Nazarene age-mates no significant differentials are evident. Therefore, explanations for the variation between the economic behavior of the Christians and the non-Christians among the Rimrock Navajos must lie in areas other than those of theological and ethical concerns.

Theological-ethical Capacities: General Functions

Theological-ethical capacities inherent in Protestantism operate effectively only as their total doctrinal framework and philosophical rationale are internalized. It is thus unlikely that their potential for affecting any type of economic change has been realized in the conversion of the Rimrock Navajos to Christianity.

The connection between the theology factor and economic change among the Rimrock Navajos has been generally limited to two areas:

1. For those initially seeking to legitimate previously adopted, novel, economic behavior, the synthesized value systems provided effective reorientation. However, I am suggesting that the nature of the novel religious systems involved in this legitimation are inconsequential. Any new ideology offering justification for rejecting old patterns would have been sufficient, be it Protestant or otherwise.

2. By its emphasis on personal responsibility in the definition of one's religious life, Christian doctrine fostered a new individualism that in some cases had an impact on economic behavior patterns.

These realized theological capacities are not generalized and have probably influenced at best only a limited number of the Nazarene Navajos. On the other hand, there appear to have been no purely religious changes in the value systems of the Mormon Navajos in the area. L.D.S. missionaries have never emphasized the need for change or theoretical realignment and, as a result, commitments by the Navajos have been rare. Again, in spite of the strong Protestant-ethic themes that often characterize Mormon messages in Anglo wards, the tendency is to deal with more basic "issues" in preaching to and teaching the Lamanites.

I am contending that there has never been any need for the Mormon Navajos to modify or accommodate, much less replace their traditional, religious value systems. Therefore, it is extremely unlikely that Christian ideological postulates per se have had any connection whatsoever with their economic behavior.

The influence of the churches' ethical proscriptions upon the economic activities of the Rimrock-Navajo Christians, while not grounded in doctrinal formulations in the typical Protestant-ethic fashion, has been more directly evident than that of the theological concerns. Nevertheless, the negatively toned moral standards have not had an economic impact of the magnitude Willems reports for that accompanying the rise of Protestantism in Brazil.[45] There, unlike the Rimrock situation, converts made a direct connection between their improved financial status and their new ethical behavior. They reasoned that:

> formerly they had spent too much money on alcohol, lottery tickets, gambling, tobacco, cosmetics, movies, and prostitution. Once they gave up these "sins," substantial amounts of money were made available for permissible and necessary things.[46]

Most of these "sins" have never been a problem for the Rimrock Navajos, with the exception of alcohol. Gambling has never been popular in the area, and items such as movies and prostitutes have never been that readily available. By their respective bans on drinking, smoking, and chewing, though, the Christian missions have enabled their converts to spend their income on more essential goods and services, although I have yet to find a single Mormon Navajo who quit drinking or smoking as a direct result of his affiliation with the Saints. Either he had not indulged previous to his baptism or he has continued, despite missionary admonitions to the contrary, to use alcohol, tobacco, or both.

Another problem that one faces in attempting to connect the ethical proscriptions of the Christian churches with any new "responsible" economic behavior is the fact that traditional, Navajo moral codes have almost identical social prohibitions. According to Ladd, the proper Navajo is not supposed to drink, kill, fight, bother other men's wives, steal, lie, gamble, or be lazy.[47] Therefore, the conscientious Navajo does not need the admonitions of the white preacher.

In general, the theological-ethical capacities of Navajo Nazarenism and Mormonism exhibit only slight potential for legitimating, accelerating, or stimulating new patterns of economic behavior in the Rimrock setting.

Impact of Protestant Ethic

A particular, historical type of theological-ethical capacity, the classic idea of the Protestant ethic has by no means been of any great significance in affecting economic behavior among Rimrock-Navajo converts to Christianity. The concept is actually of little meaning or analytical value in the attempt to explain economic change in this situation for several reasons.

Rimrock-Navajo converts have not been adequately exposed to basic Christian concepts (for example, the Mormons) or they have not sufficiently internalized critical theological categories (for example, the Nazarenes). Related to this is the fact that missionaries have not dealt effectively with specific historical and theological issues, nor have they, by their own admission, ever stressed the importance of work for work's sake, the idea of the calling extended to all areas of life, or the development of a "worldly asceticism" in which pleasurable goals are subordinated to the demands of labor and economic achievement.

Ethical precepts, although their implementation has in many cases adjusted and rationalized financial outlays, have not been directly justified by reference to classical Protestant-theological rationales. Also, the ethical demands of evangelistic Christianity are not dramatically different from those moral principles implicit in traditional Navajo life.

Again, the synthesized value systems developed by the Nazarenes have not provided a suitable theoretical framework within which to legitimate the economic demands of Weber's conception of the Protestant ethic; thus, there are none of the vital "psychological sanctions" directing the motivations of the Christian population in Rimrock that might have significant economic consequences.

Despite the emphasis the Nazarenes have placed on change, the attitude has had little significance for economic behavior. The deliberate changes themselves have been behavioral, negative, reactionary, and expressed in situations where previous nonconformity with traditional patterns has preconditioned the response. This observation is statistically supported by the fact that among first-generation sample personnel where the anti-tradition theme is most clearly manifested, economic differentials between Christians and non-Christians are the least meaningful.

In light of these limiting factors, it seems obvious that the classical notion of the Protestant ethic provides little insight into the relationship between religious change and economic behavior among the Rimrock Navajos.

Institutional Capacities

The institutional capacities of Protestantism, as they have been realized in the programs of the Mormons and the Nazarenes in Rimrock, have played a more evident role in the relationship between the religious factor and new patterns of economic behavior among the Navajos than have the theological-ethical potentials. The aspects of the programs of the Christian missions in the area that have significantly affected the economic activities of the Navajos can be divided into two main divisions: (1) the opportunities and benefits stemming from church participation; and (2) the positive results of practical admonitions and instructions from the missionaries themselves not directly related to ideological concerns.

Organizational Activities

This first type of institutional capacity operative within the structure of the Mormon and Nazarene-mission programs, which I have labeled *organizational activities,* has had a variety of direct and indirect influences on the economic behavior of the Rimrock-Navajo converts.

Both Christian-missionary organizations in the Rimrock area have been fairly consistent over the years in providing direct forms of economically significant training and assistance. In many respects, this type of activity has been the primary focus of Mormon missions among the Navajos for years.

> Missionary work in this area [Rimrock] dealt more with teaching them [the Navajos] to farm, build good homes, and keep themselves clean than in disseminating the theological precepts of Mormonism. . . . This policy is simply based on the fact that before the missionaries could improve the Indian's spiritual conditions they would have to provide the physical necessities of life.[48]

Under this persisting Mormon policy, Rimrock-Navajo men have been given practical instruction in agricultural and animal-husbandry methods. On the other hand, the women have received domestic training in a broad spectrum of the domestic arts from cooking to sewing.

The Nazarene missionaries have provided similar instructional assistance, though not under the auspices of as consistent a program as that of the Mormons. They also have got directly involved in Navajo innovative economic pursuits. For example, in the early years of the mission, Fry worked with the ambitious Navajo entrepreneurs who attempted to organize an Indian-controlled coop store in Rimrock in 1948. He donated much of his time in the attempt to keep the venture from going under, though the project failed within a year. The Nazarene workers have also encouraged their Navajo congregation to make and sell handicrafts, an effort that in past years has seen some success in generating fresh income for participating members.

Both missions have always distributed a variety of food stuffs and hardgoods directly to their Navajo membership in the Rimrock area. The Rimrock files are replete with references to incidents of gift giving by the Nazarenes: Kool-Aid, cookies, Christmas dinners, relief materials, used radios, baby shoes, toys, candy, and a variety of food and second-hand clothing. Fry recalls an annual distribution that has continued, with some modification, as a part of the Nazarene mission's direct-help program:

> At Christmas time we saw to it that each women received some dishes, knives, forks, spoons, towels, and dish cloths. The men received combs, handkerchiefs, or some useful tool.[49]

Another important area in which the Christian missions have had direct effects on the economic attitudes and performance of their Rimrock-Navajo communicants is in their general functioning as cohesive organizations. Cartwright has underscored the importance of the formal group as a medium for bringing about behavioral changes in people and has posited five "principles" defining the group's ideal role in this capacity.[50] The Rimrock missions, especially the Nazarene element, conform sufficiently to this general pattern to suggest that they have a natural potential for motivating change. Members have a strong sense of belonging, the group has an attractiveness for its members so that it can thus exert an effective influence, new programs are often related to the elements initially attracting members, the greatest intragroup influence is wielded by its prestigious members, and efforts to deviate from group norms encounter strong resistance.[51]

Initially, the Christian-mission organizations offer the Rimrock Navajos a novel social context in which those who have experienced the disruption of their traditional world can reorient and restructure personal relationships, similar to the situation Willems observed in Brazil:

> The Protestant congregation with its strong accent on intimate cooperation, personal responsibility, mutual as well as self-help, provides opportunity for the individual whose personal community has been destroyed, to "find himself." [52]

Within this type of social need, then, the fellowship of the mission develops a creative cohesiveness, and a context evolves in which both directed and nondirected change are real possibilities. For example, when the missionary instigates a program of positive economic potential that effectively captures group imagination, individual behavior patterns will be influenced. The group also acts to bring about nondirected change of economic consequence through the natural functioning of the missions' individual program styles, their assignments of responsibility, opportunities for participation, and the development of group confidence.

The church organizations of the Rimrock Navajos have always had many positions of responsibility that have been held by either appointed or elected Navajo personnel. Successful tenure in such offices—Sunday-school teacher, board member, missionary-society president—has had the effect of helping the participant adjust to the demands of industrial wage labor by giving him an understanding of what is meant by "responsibility" in a Western context. This is reflected in the higher ratings of the churched Navajos in their job efficiency and performance evaluations and in their consumer behavior.

Navajo church-goers generally emphasize the importance of participation. They like to sing, testify, help make policy decisions, and hold organizational offices. In fact, many of the Nazarenes who have shifted their allegiance to the Pentecostal sect explain their actions on that basis. As one defector argued: "I don't just like to sit all the time and listen to the same old preacher stand up and talk to me. I like to take part in what's going on."

Participation in the fellowship of the church, similar to the assignment of responsibility, has had a broad impact on the behavior of the Rimrock-Navajo converts. Bertha Yazi has expressed the feeling that the opportunities for participation in the mission lie at the base of the churched Navajos' greater assertiveness in community activities, and efficiency and innovativeness in job performance.

> The people here [the church people] talk a lot. I mean, during the years they've come to the point where they say a few things, maybe read the Bible in church or something, and then they talk together and discuss things. The other people, they would hardly ever get together unless there was a squaw dance, but that's nothing formal; I mean, nothing where everybody can participate in the one thing they're doing. They must have the dance over there and maybe the feeding over here or something, where . . . if they go to church, they say, "Come to church at six o'clock to ten o'clock," and everybody goes there and participates. Then say at the noon hour, they talk and . . . just get together. But, this other group, they're still shy, and . . . they don't talk in public, just two or three people maybe, that would have anything to say, especially the womenfolks. They would never have anything to say unless they had been going to church; then they would have something to say. . . .
> These other people are used to talking and can get together and maybe plan things; whereas the other group, that has never gone to church are over there all by themselves and they don't really know how to take each other or talk with each other, or they don't know how to carry on.

Group participation in mission activities has also had other practical results. For example, in 1970, a Navajo reading class at the Nazarene mission was the setting for a discussion about "seeing" difficulties, and, as a direct result, the group, mostly ladies, went to the Public Health Service hospital in Blackrock and had their eyes checked. Several of the women were soon wearing prescription lenses provided by the service.

Both the Nazarenes and the Mormons have offered unique educational opportunities for their Rimrock-Navajo converts.

The Saints have a "placement program" under which a Navajo student is sent to another community, usually in Utah, where he lives with an Anglo-Mormon family and attends a local public school. While this particular phase of Mormon activity has been criticized by various Indian pressure groups recently, it has provided a beneficial service for many Mormon Navajos, especially in the days when educational opportunities for The People in Rimrock were severely limited. Recently, the Mormons have been encouraging their Navajo membership to send their children to Brigham Young University, the cultural citadel of Mormondom, and in 1970 three Navajo students from Rimrock were attending the school in Provo, Utah.

The Nazarenes have had a Bible school in Albuquerque for the past twenty years, and up until 1970 its high-school facilities were accredited. Many Navajo members of the Rimrock-Nazarene mission have sent their children to the Albuquerque institute. The Nazarenes also have several church-related colleges where five of the local Navajos have, with financial aid from the church, received from one to four years of higher education.

The Nazarenes have also placed a strong emphasis on literacy. In the early years of the mission in Rimrock the Wycliff Bible Translators helped the missionaries structure a Navajo reading program that is still an important phase of local church activities.

Both Christian missions have long offered their memberships travel opportunities not available to the nonchurched group among the Rimrock Navajos. The Mormons have sponsored and encouraged numerous trips to such places as Salt Lake City and the temple in Mesa, Arizona, besides persuading Navajo youth to go on "missions" to other areas in the Southwest. Similarly, the Nazarenes have always taken many of their Navajo converts to the district assemblies in various cities in New Mexico, Arizona, and California. The missionaries have on several occasions also taken members from the Rimrock organization to churches in other parts of the country in order to put "the results of their work among the Indians" on display.

A new form of economic behavior introduced by both churches, though actually only effective among the Nazarenes, is the tithe. A good mission member is expected to contribute ten percent of his income to the organizational cause. According to actual figures, the Rimrock Nazarenes give approximately three percent of their total-cash income, a figure slightly lower than the per capita giving among Anglo Nazarenes. While direct results from the gift are assumed to take the shape of intangible blessings, many of the converts rationalize the new expense with the observation that previous to their church commitment they had annually expended large amounts of money for ceremonial expenses.

Implicitly, for most of the Navajo Christians, the tithe is an investment in a new, supposedly more effective, method of health maintenance with occasional economic benefits. For this reason, few offerings are ever given with any attitude of personal sacrifice, despite the instruction of the missionaries.

Another important function served by the organizational activities of the missions in the area is the immediate contact situation it provides. The church, through its several programs, gives the participating Navajo a direct exposure to many elements of white life and, in the case of the Mormons, an opportunity to develop personal ties and contacts with Anglos that often result in economic reward : financial aid, a better job, agricultural assistance, and instruction.

Practical Admonitions

The Christian missionary, during his tenure among the Rimrock Navajos, has generally felt that he has a certain responsibility for the material as well as the spiritual well-being of his congregation. Some of the efforts in this direction have been channeled through different aspects of the mission program. On the other hand, many of the missionary's attempts to improve the physical circumstances of the membership have been less formally structured, essentially verbal, and normally expressed in a "personal-advise" type of framework. These direct efforts to influence behavioral change in nonreligious areas through rational persuasion, I am labeling *practical admonitions*.

The practical admonition is different than the ethical proscription of the classic Protestant ethic for several reasons: it is positive rather than negative; it has an explicit rather than an implicit significance for behavioral changes in nonideological contexts; it is more directly related to secular Western values; and it does not have a doctrinally defined theological orientation, being framed instead in the personal biases and concerns of the individual missionary.

One of the persistent themes in the practical admonitions of the Rimrock missionaries is the notion that cleanliness is a fundamental value in defining the good life. Suggesting that "cleanliness is next to godliness," the Nazarene workers in particular have encouraged the Navajo to wash and change their clothes more often, clean their houses, wash themselves and their children regularly, and if possible, build a frame house with a wooden floor to expedite the cleaning process.

Because of the limited employment possibilities in Rimrock, many of the Navajo Christians have ben encouraged by their missionaries to migrate to a potentially more prosperous area. In several cases, missionaries have made arrangements for their parishioners to take jobs elsewhere and have even helped them move and get established in the new locations.

Both the Nazarene and the Mormon missionaries have stressed the importance of education. Whenever possible, they have tried to demonstrate this and in individual cases have helped to expedite educational opportunities. Likewise, they have encouraged the Navajos to develop and improve English language skills.

These, along with other less significant practical admonitions, have had a direct impact on the economic behavior patterns of the Rimrock-Navajo converts, witnessed in many cases by their own admission. However, what about the value orientations that motivate the Indians to heed and make operational this constructive advice?

Peacock has argued that "in order to have direct instructions take effect they must be framed in some type of cosmic scheme or belief system."[53] While this *may* be the case with the Rimrock Navajos, it is difficult to isolate or substantiate those systems.

In the first place, the missionaries themselves render a range of personally devised rationales to justify their admonitions, with or without theological orientations. For example, Rockford explained his emphasis on cleanliness by simply observing: "These Indians just aren't going to make it these days if they don't clean up." On the other hand, Fry attempted to legitimate the advice from a biblical perspective:

> Jesus said, "Seek ye first the kingdom of God and His righteousness and all these things shall be added unto you." To my way of reasoning, when God saves a man or woman and they are really born again, they receive the inward cleansing of the Holy Spirit coming into their lives. This also results in an outward cleansing, which they do themselves because of the inward cleansing. This conversion changes their whole outlook on life. They become new men and women, and there comes a desire to live a clean moral life, this results in outward cleansing, too.[54]

Nevertheless, the Navajo converts explain their implementation of these admonitive propositions from their Anglo leadership on the basis of entirely different rationales. While one might expect them to relate the advice to the premises of their synthesized, ideological value scheme, their logic tends instead to be more realistic, oriented toward immediate needs and this-worldly concerns. For example, Charles Yazi gave me the following reason for using English:

> What I read in the Bible says that Jesus, "When about I'm coming back to this world they just be more and more just one language, like way back in the Old Testament." In the Old

Testament it tells about when we had one language. . . . It's going to be one language. . . .

Now, every Indian, where ever I go, in California, some other states; where ever I go, the little children, they talks English. . . . Here, just my family here, they don't use the Navajo language now. We just use English all the time. . . . It's going to be one language now.

This explanation is typical of those one usually receives from the Navajo Christians when asking them to explain their non-traditional behavior. While many will admit that certain ideas were initially defined for them by the missionary, the rationales legitimizing their actual adoption and implementation are generally unique from that characterizing the notion's original context. This is not to say that the logic employed by the Navajo converts does not have a certain regularity. On the contrary, two basic themes are persistently evident in the reasons they give for their individual behavioral modifications; a pragmatic realism, and an urgent sense of survival.

The Navajo has often been characterized as a very practical individual who carefully analyzes novel ideas with a rational selectiveness. Ladd has concluded that the Navajo is very much of an empiricist and "always ready to try something new."[55]

For this reason, when the Navajo encounters a new item or concept that is functionally superior to an older form, he does not necessarily wait to adopt it until he has reordered his whole value system. For example, give him a pickup truck and, though he has been driving a horse and wagon for years, the immediately evident advantages will provide any schematic justification that might be needed. While this may not always be the case in areas where relative merits are not as clearly defined, the Navajos make many decisions, especially where economic well-being is concerned, that need no ultimate legitimation beyond the primary pragmatic value itself.

The second theme that pervades the reasons the Rimrock-Navajo Christians use to explain their unique behavioral patterns is an anxious will to survive. Education, special training, mobility, wage incomes, and language facility are simply means whereby one can escape the disruption of the old world and prepare himself for the new. The urgency of this theme as it is expressed by individual Navajos is generally related to the degree of social maladjustment in each case. In line with Rapoport's causative explanation that "conversion to Christianity is . . . a response to sociocultural disorganization and emotional need,"[56] I am suggesting that the anxiety underlying the churched Navajo's abnormal sense of survival is a product, ultimately, of the desire for meaningful social reorientation. Again, the demands posed by the disruption of the individual's framework of social relationships themselves provides adequate legitimation for the adoption of new patterns of behavior that promise a meaningful restructuring of his personal community.

In general, then, it seems that the Navajo convert's acceptance and implementation of practical instruction by the missionaries, both Mormon and Nazarene, does not necessitate a theoretical orientation in any "cosmic system," modified or otherwise. Rather it is legitimated by its own immediate value or by the social adjustment potential it represents. This conclusion is reinforced by the fact that the Mormon Navajos, even though their traditional belief systems have not been altered by Christian theological principles, respond to precisely the same type of opportunities and admonitions accepted and implemented by the more iconoclastic Nazarenes.

Institutional Capacities: General Functions

The institutional capacities of the Nazarenes and Mormon missions to the Rimrock Navajos have been directly instrumental in the legitimation, acceleration, and stimulation of new patterns of economic behavior among the converts. For those with previously adopted styles of nonconforming economic behavior, the church fellowship offered a new social orientation in which individual acquisitiveness was not disruptive. Others found opportunities in the church to reinforce already existing tendencies toward economic rationalism. For example, those adopting more effective methods of agriculture and animal husbandry found in the church additional opportunities for instruction and training. For many wage-working Navajos, the mission context was an adjustment mechanism and an effective buffer between his traditional environment and the white man's world in which he worked. In many other cases, the institutional capacities of the religious organizations in the area manifested themselves through their formative and accelerative effects on economic behavior as the missions presented novel opportunities, benefits, and practical assistance to their Navajo participants.

The importance of the institutional capacities of Protestantism in the definition of the relationship between religious change and economic behavior among the Rimrock Navajos is demonstrated by the following observations:

1. The inherent weaknesses of the theological-ethical capacities of Protestantism, and concomitantly the Protestant ethic, as they are manifested in the religious-change situation of the Rimrock Navajos are of little explanatory value.

2. The Mormon Navajos, despite their very clear lack of ideological change or adjustment, still exhibit an economic rationalism comparable to that of the Nazarenes. Again, Mormon children grow up under the same general ideological influence as do the traditional youth, yet in later years they significantly outperform them economically.

3. Most of the factors originally disposing Navajos to Christianity can be classed as nonideological. For example, Hughes posits fourteen factors underlying the religious-change experience of the Navajo women who affiliated with the Nazarene church. Of this total, eleven of the reasons were nonideological.[57]

4. By nature, the Navajo tends to be very pragmatic and realistic in responding to innovative-change pressures.[58]

5. The historical fact that organizational programs and practical admonitions originating in the mission centext have been direct in overtly encouraging economic change.

"Hanging around" at the rodeo.

"Busting" a bronc at the rodeo.

RELIGIOUS CHANGE AND ECONOMIC BEHAVIOR:
A MEANINGFUL RELATIONSHIP

The uniform modes of the relationship between the religious factor and economic behavior among the Navajos in Rimrock have been established. They have been defined specifically in terms of the institutional capacities of the Christian-missionary programs that have been and still are functioning in the area.

The classic concept of the Protestant ethic, defined by Weber as a significant force in the development of economic rationalism in the rise of Western capitalism, is of little meaning within the context of Rimrock's religious change situation. While Christian missions have had an influence on economic change among the Navajos, it has been the result of organizational activities and practical programs rather than of the replacement of traditional-belief systems with Western theology.

For this reason, it can be concluded that the role of the Christian missions among the Rimrock Navajos in affecting economic change has been merely one of presenting additional, practical options to members of their congregations. Peter Antonio and other of his tribesmen have prospered as a result of their ability to simply take selective advantage of these benefits.

NOTES

1. H. G. Barnett, *Innovation: The Basis of Cultural Change* (New York: McGraw-Hill, 1953), p. 15.

2. Vogt, "Navajo Veterans," p. 117.

3. Barnett, *Innovations*, p. 378.

4. Vogt, "Navajo Veterans," p. 118.

5. Clyde Kluckhohn, "The Philsophy of the Navajo Indians," in *Ideological Differences and World Order,* ed. F. S. C. Northrop (New Haven, Connecticut: Yale University Press, 1949), p. 376.

6. Ibid.

7. Rapoport, p. 58.

8. Ibid., p. 74.

9. Hughes, p. 35.

10. Rapaport, pp. 71–77; Hughes, pp. 114–128.

11. Rapoport, p. 73; H. G. Barnett, "Personal Conflicts and Cultural Change," *Social Forces* 20 (1941):170.

12. Alexander Gerschendron, "The Modernization of Entrepreneurship," in *Modernization: The Dynamics of Growth,* ed. Myron Weiner (New York: Basic Books, 1966); Kurt Samuelsson, *Religion and Economic Action,* trans. E. G. French (Stockholm: Scandanavian University Press, 1961).

13. Stanislav Andreski, "Method and Substantive Theory in Max Weber," in *The Protestant Ethic and Modernization,* ed. S. N. Eisenstadt (New York: Basic Books, 1968), pp. 46–63; James L. Peacock, "Religion, Communication, and Modernization: A Weberian Critique of Some Recent Views," *Human Organization* 28, no. 1 (1969):35–41.

14. Andreski, p. 59.

15. Reinhard Bendix, "A Case Study in Cultural and Educational Mobility: Japan and the Protestant Ethic," in *Social Structure and Mobility in Economic Development,* eds. Neil J. Smelser and Seymour Martin Lipset (Chicago: Aldine Publishing Company, 1966), p. 263.

16. Eisenstadt, p. 8.

17. This distinction is comparable to that made by Hughes in separating the practical or applied aspects of Nazarenism from the ideological or spiritual phases of its program; *see* Hughes, "The Navajo Woman and Nazarene Christianity."

18. Weber, pp. 128–43.

19. Ibid., p. 138.

20. Church of the Nazarene, *Manual* (Kansas City, Missouri: Nazarene Publishing House, 1968), p. 31.

21. O'Dea, p. 29.

22. Hughes, p. 87.

23. Kluckhohn, "The Rimrock Navajo," p. 337.

24. Rapoport, p. 52.

25. John Ladd, *The Structure of a Moral Code* (Cambridge, Massachusetts: Harvard University Press, 1957), p. 205.

26. Kluckhohn, "The Philosophy of the Navajo Indians," p. 370.

27. Vine Deloria, Jr., *Custer Died for Your Sins* (New York: Avon Books, 1969), p. 126.

28. For further discussion of the general language problem in the Navajo religious-change situation, see David Aberle, *The Peyote Religion among the Navajo* (Chicago: Aldine Publishing Company, 1966), pp. 376–79; Rapoport, pp. 137–38.

29. Ibid., p. 137.

30. Karl Barth, *Evangelical Theology: An Introduction* (New York: Holt, Rinehart, and Winston, 1963), p. 10.

31. Reichard, "The Navajo and Christianity," p. 67.

32. Ladd, p. 204.

33. Ibid.

34. Reichard, "The Navajo and Christianity," pp. 68–69.

35. Leland C. Wyman, W. W. Hill, and I. Osinai, "Navajo Eschatology," *University of New Mexico Bulletin* 4, no. 1 (1942):37.

36. Reichard, "The Navajo and Christianity," p. 67.

37. Blanchard, "Religious Change and Economic Behavior," p. 391.

38. Weber, p. 98.

39. Bendix, p. 265.

40. Church of the Nazarene, *Manual*, p. 31.

41. Reichard, "The Navajo and Christianity,," p. 71.

42. Kluckhohn, "The Rimrock Navajo," p. 337.

43. Katherine Spencer, "Mythology and Values: An Analysis of Navajo-Chantway Myths," *Memoirs of the American Folklore Society* 48 (1957):86

44. Hughes, p. 102.

45. Emilio Willems, "Culture Change and the Rise of Protestantism in Brazil and Chile," in *The Protestant Ethic and Modernization,* ed. S. N. Eisenstadt (New York: Basic Books, 1968), p. 197.

46. Ibid., p. 198.

47. Ladd, p. 252.

48. Flake, pp. 12–13.

49. Reverend Fry, personal communication, 1970.

50. Dorwin Cartwright, "Achieving Change in People: Some Applications of Group Dynamics Theory," in *Organizational Behavior and Human Performance,* eds L. L. Cummings and W. E. Scott (Homewood, Illinois: Richard D. Irwin and The Dorsey Press, 1969), pp. 727–29.

51. Ibid.

52. Willems, *Followers,* p. 123.

53. James Peacock, personal communication, 1971.

54. Reverend Fry, personal communication, 1970.

55. Ladd, pp. 205–206.

56. Rapoport, p. 77.

57. Hughes, pp. 146–59.

58. Ladd, p. 205.

5

Conclusion

SUMMARY

The Rimrock-Navajo community has changed dramatically in recent years. Significantly, it has developed a new awareness of its identity as a group, and relationships with local Anglos have begun to be tempered by a new balance of power.

The Rimrock Navajos have grown increasingly dependent on wage incomes and government assistance. A growing population, coupled with a decline in the productivity of the land and customary methods of livelihood, has accelerated the modification of traditional patterns of economic behavior. These changes reflect tendencies toward a generalized economic rationalism.

Both the Nazarene and the Mormon missionaries have been active among the Rimrock Navajos in the past two decades. By 1970, there were about 400 of the Navajos who were fairly active in the missions, the great majority of this number participating in the programs of the Nazarene organization.

223

In the comparison of the economic behavior of those individuals who were active in the missions with that of the nonchurched elements, it is obvious that the churched Navajos in Rimrock demonstrate a significantly greater rationality in their economic activities. They have more education, special training, jobs, income, consistent consumer habits, and higher job performance and efficiency ratings.

The significant differences in behavior between the Christian and the non-Christian groups raises the question of the specific influence of religious change in the development of economic rationalism. Weber's classic treatment of the Protestant ethic's effect on the rise of capitalism,[1] as it is modified by Eisenstadt's concept of "transformative capacities" and focused on a limited cultural situation,[2] provides an adequate theoretical framework.

In order to deal with the problem of religious change and economic behavior, a general theory of change is needed. Change is defined as an individual process, the subject moving from psychological receptivity and the availability of novel alternatives through a complex and extended period of internalization. Value systems go through this pattern of modification, but ideological values adjust more slowly than others. For this reason, the gaps between religious behavior and its underlying values tend to outdistance those characterizing the same relationship in other areas of cultural behavior.

The following observations have been made :

1. In general, the churched factions among the Rimrock Navajos tend to do better economically than the nonchurched.

2. In terms of the qualities defining Weber's ideal types —economic traditionalism and economic rationalism—the overall development of the Rimrock-Navajo community, consistent with its general acculturative process, has been in the direction of the latter, more modern tendency.[3] However, it is also clear that the Christian Navajos have been moving toward that rational ideal at a faster rate than the non-Christian faction.

3. The members of the Rimrock mission have not been adequately internalizing basic Christian concepts, so, despite

the historical Protestant-ethic orientation of the Nazarene and Mormon churches, the theological precepts underlying Weber's classic concept have not become operational among the Navajo converts. This failure is due both to the natural resistance of traditional patterns and language as well as the ineffectiveness of missionary methods.

4. In the process of religious change, traditional ideological value systems of the Rimrock Navajos are not being replaced nor even dramatically altered by Christian theological tenets. Rather, the converts are synthesizing elements of their customary thought patterns and implicit philosophical premises with selected elements of the new doctrines. This accommodation legitimates certain new behaviors without, in most cases, seriously modifying traditional belief systems. Therefore, the event of a Navajo's rejecting traditional religious activities and joining a Chrstian congregation is actually not as "radical" or "surprising" as some anthropologists have previously suggested.[4]

5. The theological-ethical capacities of Protestantism, as they have been expressed in the Rimrock context, have exercised only a very insignificant influence on Navajo economic behavior. Therefore, the classic notion of the Protestant ethic provides little theoretical leverage in this case for understanding the relationship between religious and economic change, and is only of slight meaning in this particular context.

6. The institutional capacities of Protestantism in the Rimrock area have had noticeable effects on the economic styles of the Navajos, manifesting their potential by means of the organizational activities of the missions and the practical admonitions of their leadership.

7. The primary role of the Christian missions among the Rimrock Navajos in their influence on economic behavior has been one of merely presenting new practical options to their converts.

PROJECTIONS

Religious change in the Rimrock area has had its economic effects, but the Protestant ethic, as it has been defined historically, has been of only limited significance. This suggests that the religious or theological context circumscribing the institutional life of the Christian missions among the Rimrock Navajos has been practically incidental in the economic-change process. It thus seems that a secular organization with similar opportunities and institutional characteristics could have stimulated a comparable development toward economic rationalism without a theology or an evangelistic commitment.

The future of the churches' roles in economic development among the Rimrock Navajos appears to be of diminishing importance. Perhaps, similar to the Brazilian situation, new religious forces will grow continually less effective in the acculturative process:

> If may be argued that further secularization accompanying upward mobility will gradually reduce and eventually extinguish the role of the historical churches as factors of culture change.[5]

In Rimrock, signs of this process are already evident. Many of the Navajos in the age group from twenty to forty who have been raised in the church, particularly the Nazarene organization, and who have obtained an education and either secured a good job locally or have migrated away from the community, are gradually loosening their ties with the Christian institutions. It appears that, while it is not yet the general rule, with increased acculturation, the tendency for secularity to accompany economic achievement will be reinforced. Also, with increased government spending, tribal programs, educational opportunities, and general economic development in the Rimrock area, the importance of the organizational life and beneficial options afforded by the Nazarene and Mormon programs will become increasingly less significant. Once they have lost their economic function, and this appears imminent, missionary efforts in the area will die, appealing to only a handful of those remaining "misfits" and "malcontents."

The Charles Yazi's, the Juan Begay's, and the Peter Antonio's will eventually see their children rejecting the tenets and institutional programs of the missions. Increasingly, young people in the area, no longer dependent on the second-hand clothes, broken dishes, and Kool-Aid doled out by condescending whites, will turn to religious forms more consistent with the realities of Navajo life. The nickle-and-dime benefits of Protestant affiliation will have lost their appeal, and dusty pews, dirty hymnbooks, and discarded Bibles will invoke only memories of those few years when sainthood was a profitable enterprise in Rimrock.

NOTES

1. Weber.
2. Eisenstadt, p. 10.
3. Weber, pp. 59–75.
4. Hughes, p. 102; Reichard, "The Navajo and Christianity," p. 66.
5. Willems, "Culture Change and the Rise of Protestantism," p. 208.

Selected Bibliography

Aberle, David. 1961. Navajo. In *Matrilineal kinship,* eds. David M. Schneider and Kathleen Gough, pp. 96–201. Berkeley and Los Angeles : University of California Press.

———. 1966. *The peyote religion among the Navajo.* Chicago : Aldine Publishing Company.

Adair, John, and Vogt, Evon Z. 1949. Navajo and Zuni veterans : a study in contrasting modes of culture change. *American Anthropologist* 51 :547–61.

Andreski, Stanislav. 1968. Method and substantive theory in Max Weber. In *The Protestant ethic and modernization,* ed. S. N. Eisenstadt, pp. 46–63. New York : Basic Books.

Barnett, H. G. 1941. Personal conflicts and cultural change. *Social Forces* 20 :160–71.

———. 1953. *Innovation: the basis of cultural change.* New York : McGraw-Hill.

Barth, Karl. 1963. *Evangelical theology: an introduction.* New York : Holt, Rinehart, and Winston.

Bellah, Robert N. 1957 *Tokugawa religion.* Glencoe, Illinois : The Free Press.

———. 1967. Religious systems. In *People of Rimrock,* eds. Evon

Z. Vogt and Ethel M. Albert, pp. 227–64. Cambridge, Massachusetts : Harvard University Press.

Bendix, Reinhard. 1960. *Max Weber: an intellectual portrait.* New York : Doubleday.

———. 1966. A case study in cultural and educational mobility : Japan and the Protestant ethic. In *Social structure and mobility in economic development,* eds. Neil J. Smelser and Seymour Martin Lipset, pp. 262–79. Chicago : Aldine Publishing Company.

Blanchard, Kendall A. 1971. Religious change and economic behavior among the Rimrock Navajo. Ph.D. dissertation, Southern Methodist University.

———. 1971. *The Rimrock Navajos: a growing sense of community in historical perspective.* Navajo Historical Series, no. 1. Window Rock, Arizona : The Navajo Tribe.

———. 1975. Changing sex roles and Protestantism among Navajo women in Rimrock. *Journal for the Scientific Study of Religion* 14 :43–50.

Bureau of Indian Affairs. 1970. Reservation Population support capacity study. Window Rock, Arizona : Navajo Tribe. Mimeographed.

Burling, Robbins. 1962. Maximization theories and the study of economic anthropology. *American Anthropologist* 64 :802–821.

Cartwright, Dorwin. 1969. Achieving change in people : some applications of group dynamics theory. In *Organizational behavior and human performance,* eds. L. L. Cummings and W. E. Scott, pp. 722–31. Homewood, Illinois : Richard D. Irwin and The Dorsey Press.

Church of the Nazarene. 1944–1971. Minutes : North American Indian district assembly. Kansas City, Missouri : Nazarene Publishing House.

———. 1950–1971. *Voice of the Redman.* Kansas City, Missouri : Nazarene Publishing House.

———. 1968. *Manual.* Kansas City, Missouri : Nazarene Publishing House.

Deloria, Vine, Jr. 1969. *Custer died for your sins*. New York : Avon Books.

Eisenstadt, S. N. 1968. The Protestant-ethic thesis in an analytical and comparative framework. In *The Protestant ethic and modernization*, ed. Eisenstadt, pp. 3–45. New York : Basic Books.

Fischoff, Ephraim. 1968. The Protestant ethic and the spirit of capitalism : the history of a controversy. In *The Protestant ethic and modernization*, ed. S. N. Eisenstadt, pp. 67–86. New York : Basic Books.

Flake, David Kay. 1965. A history of Mormon missionary work with the Hopi, Navajo, and Zuni Indians. Masters thesis, Brigham Young University.

Geertz, Clifford. 1968. Religious belief and economic behavior in a central Javanese town. In *The Protestant ethic and modernization*, ed. S. N. Eisenstadt, pp. 309–342. New York : Basic Books.

———, ed. 1968. *The Protestant ethic and modernization*. New York. Basic Books.

Gerschendron, Alexander. 1966. The modernization of entrepreneurship. In *Modernization: the dynamics of growth*, ed. Myron Weiner, pp. 246–57. New York : Basic Books.

Hammond, George D., and Rey, Agapito. 1929. *Expedition into New Mexico made by Antonio de Espejo, 1582–1583, as revealed in the journal of Diego Perez de Luxan, a member of the party*. Los Angeles : Quivaro Society.

Harrington, John P. 1940. Southern peripheral Athapaskan origins, divisions, and migrations. *Smithsonian Institute Miscellaneous Collections* 100 :503–532.

Hill, W. W. 1938 The agricultural and hunting methods of the Navajo Indians. *Yale University Publications in Anthropology*, no. 18.

Hobson, Richard. 1954. Navajo acquisitive values. *Peabody Museum Papers* 42 ,no. 3.

Hughes, Charles E. 1951. The Navajo woman and Nazarene Christianity. Honors thesis, Harvard University.

Indian Claims Commission. 1970. Navajo plaintiff exhibit 3047 through 3069A, docket 229. Window Rock, Arizona : Navajo Tribe. Mimeographed.

———. 1970. Navajo land claim, docket 229. Window Rock, Arizona : Navajo Tribe. Mimeographed.

Kluckhohn, Clyde. 1927. *To the foot of the rainbow.* New York : Century.

———. 1944. *Navajo witchcraft.* Boston : Beacon Press.

———., and Leighton. Dorothea C. 1946. *The Navajo.* 1962 edition. Garden City, New York : Doubleday.

———. 1949. The·philosophy of the Navajo Indians. In *Ideological differences and world order,* ed. F. S. C. Northrop pp. 356–83. New Haven, Connecticut : Yale University Press.

———. 1949. The Rimrock project. In Alexander Leighton and Dorothea C. Leighton, Gregario, the hand-trembler. *Peabody Museum Papers* 40, no. 1 : 6–11.

———. 1952. Values and value-orientations in the theory of action : an exploration in definition and classification. In *Toward a general theory of action,* eds. Talcott Parsons and Edward A. Shils, pp. 388–433. Cambridge, Massachusetts : Harvard University Press.

———. 1956. Aspects of the demographic history of a small population. In *Estudios Anthropologicos,* ed. Juan Comas, pp. 359–79. Mexico City : Dirreccion General de Publicaciones.

———. 1966. The Rimrock Navajo. *Bureau of American Ethnology Bulletin* 196 :327–77.

Kluckhohn, Florence, and Strodtbeck, Fred L. 1961. *Variations in value orientation: a theory tested in five cultures.* Evanston, Illinois : Row, Peterson, and Co.

Ladd, John. 1957. *The structure of a moral code.* Cambridge, Massachusetts : Harvard University Press.

Landgraf, John L. 1954. Land-use in the Rimrock area of New Mexico. *Peabody Museum Papers* 42, no. 1.

Leighton, Alexander H., and Leighton, Dorothea C. 1944. *The Navajo door.* Cambridge, Massachusetts : Harvard University Press.

————. 1949. Gregario, the hand-trembler. *Peabody Museum Papers* 40, no. 1.

Leighton, Dorothea C., and Kluckhohn, Clyde. 1948. *Children of The People*. Cambridge, Massachusetts : Harvard University Press.

McClelland, David C. 1961. *The achieving society*. New York : Free Press.

Morgan, Kenneth. 1968. A genetic demography of a small Navajo community. Ph.D. dissertation, University of Michigan.

O'Dea, Thomas F. 1957. *The Mormons*. Chicago : University of Chicago Press.

Pauker, Guy J. 1967. Political structure. In *People of Rimrock,* eds. Evon Z. Vogt and Ethel M. Albert, pp. 191–226. Cambridge, Massachusetts : Harvard University Press.

Peacock, James L. 1969. Religion, communication, and modernization : a Weberian critique of some recent views. *Human Organization* 28, no. 1 :35–41.

Rapoport, Robert N. 1954. Changing Navajo religious values. *Peabody Museum Papers* 41, no. 2

Reichard, Gladys. 1949. The Navajo and Christianity, *American Anthropologist* 51 :66–71.

————. 1951. *Navajo religion*. New York : Bollingen Foundation.

Reynolds, T. R.; Lamphere, L.; and Cook, C. E., Jr. 1967. Time, resources, and authority in a Navajo community. *American Anthropologist* 69 :188–99.

Rimrock Project. 1939–1955. Rimrock files. Unpublished materials on file at the Laboratory of Anthropology, Santa Fe, New Mexico.

Rimrock Ward, 1871–1971. Rimrock ward historical record. Unpublished documents. Rimrock, New Mexico : Rimrock Church of Jesus Christ of Latter Day Saints.

————. 1950–1970. Rimrock Indian branch historical record. Unpublished documents. Rimrock, New Mexico : Rimrock Church of Jesus Christ of Latter Day Saints.

Roberts, John M. 1951. Three Navajo households. *Peabody Museum Papers*. 40, no. 3.

St. John, Marion. 1952. Zuni, Navajo, and Spanish-American economies. Unpublished manuscript, Harvard University.

Samuelsson, Kurt. 1961. *Religion and economic action.* Translated by E. G. French. Stockholm : Scandinavian University Press.

Smith, Joseph. 1902. *History of the Church of Jesus Christ of Latter Day Saints.* edited by B. H. Roberts. Vol. 4. Salt Lake City : Deseret Book Company.

Son of Former Many Beads. 1949. *The Rimrock Navajos.* Translated by Robert W. Young. Navajo Historical Series, No. 1. Window Rock, Arizona : The Navajo Tribe.

Spencer, Katherine. 1957. Mythology and values : an analysis of Navajo-Chantway myths. *Memoirs of the American Folklore Society* 48.

Spuhler, J. N., and Kluckhohn, Clyde. 1953. Inbreeding coefficients of the Rimrock-Navajo population. *Human Biology* 25 : 295–317.

Stokes, M. A., and Smiley, T. L. 1966. Tree-ring dates from the Navajo land claim, III. The southern sector. *Tree-Ring Bulletin* 27 : 3–4, 9–10.

Talmadge, James E. 1924. *A Study of the articles of faith.* Salt Lake City : Deseret Book Company.

Telling, Irving. 1939. History of Rimrock, New Mexico. Unpublished manuscript, Harvard University.

Vestal, Paul A. 1952. Ethnobotany of the Rimrock Navajo. *Peabody Museum Papers* 40, no. 4.

Vogt, Evon Z. 1951. Navajo veterans. *Peabody Museum Papers* 41, no. 1.

———. 1967. Ecology and economy. In *People of Rimrock,* eds. E. Z. Vogt and E. M. Albert, pp. 160–90. Cambridge, Massachusetts : Harvard University Press.

——— and Albert, Ethel M. 1967. The "comparative study of values in five cultures" project. In *People of Rimrock,* eds. Vogt and Albert, pp. 1–33. Cambridge, Massachusetts : Harvard University Press.

——— and Albert, Ethel M. eds. 1967. *People of Rimrock.* Cambridge, Massachusetts : Harvard University Press.

Walker, Deward, 1968. *Conflict and schism in Nez Perce accultura-tion*. Pullman, Washington: Washington State University Press.

Weber, Max. 1904. *The Protestant ethic and the spirit of capitalism*. Translated by Talcott Parsons. 1968 edition. New York: Scribners.

Willems, Emilio. 1967. *Followers of the new faith*. Nashville, Tennessee: Vanderbilt University Press.

———. 1968. Culture change and the rise of Protestantism in Brazil and Chile. In *The Protestant ethic and modernization*, ed. S. N. Eisenstadt, pp. 184–210. New York: Basic Books.

Witherspoon, Gary. 1970. A new look at Navajo social organization. *American Anthropologist* 72:55–65.

Worchester, Donald E. 1951. The Navajo during the Spanish regime in New Mexico. *New Mexico Historical Review* 26, no. 2:103.

Wyman, Leland C. 1950. The religion of the Navajo Indians. In *Ancient religions*, ed. Vergilius Ferm, pp. 343–61. New York: Citadel Press.

———; Hill, W. W.; and Osinai, I. 1942. Navajo eschatology. *University of New Mexico Bulletin* 4, no. 1.

Young, Robert W. 1949. Introduction. In *The Rimrock Navajos*, Son of Former Many Beads. Navajo Historical Series, no. 1.

———. 1961. *The Navajo Yearbook*. Window Rock, Arizona: Navajo Agency.

——— and Morgan, William. 1969. *The Navajo language*. Salt Lake City: Deseret Book Company.

Index

237